Joyce Wither

MW01710960

Bought at Massey Museum ~ July 6/0020

OF TURNIPS AND TEAS AND THRESHING BEES:

My Experience of the Depression Years

By Verna Thaxter

Published by
Highway Book Shop
Cobalt, Ontario
P0J 1C0

ISBN 0-88954-422-0

National Library of Canada Cataloguing in Publication Data

Thaxter, Verna, 1916-
Of turnips and teas and threshing bees : my experience of the depression years

ISBN 0-88954-422-0

1. Thaxter, Verna, 1916- . Childhood and youth. 2. Thaxter, Verna, 1916- . Family. 3. Farm life--Ontario--Spanish Region--Anecdotes. 4. Spanish Region (Ont.)--Social life and customs. 5. Spanish Region (Ont.)--Biography. I. Title.

S522.C3T48 2001 971.3'13203'092 C2001-902268-9

TOPICS

RECOLLECTIONS

The days, the weeks, and then the years,
Full of laughter, happiness, and sometimes tears.
I look in the mirror and what do I see?
Surely that old woman can't be me!
Where is that girl with the swinging pace,
Unlined skin and youthful face?
Wherever she is the years only know
Time is her enemy, the years her foe.

She was always moving, there were things to do,
One job done, then a dozen or two.
Over the years her pace is slow
Her youthful skin has lost its glow
Her face is wrinkled from all the fray,
But she doesn't regret for she's paid her way.
She still is happy and laughter is there,
She lives alone but has much less care.

Still finding those dozens of jobs to be done
Catching up on these is not much fun.
There is a son, a daughter, grandchildren too
And in-laws, of course, to increase the crew.
There are friends galore to meet and talk
Play bridge, or euchre or even walk.
Knitting, crocheting, computer too
Never at loss for things to do.

The memory is less but it does her well
It can be retrieved whenever there's a story to tell.
The more she writes, the memories flow,
She will continue to write as long as they grow.
This is a labour of love to all of you,
Enjoy this book, as she hopes you do.
She's counted her blessings and wants you to know
The older she gets the more they grow.

MOTHER

MY MOTHER

My mother was born in 1880. She was the second child of six sisters and two brothers. They lived on a farm a few miles from Parry Sound. I know little of her childhood, except that as any other farm raised child, she knew the meaning of work.

When just in her teens, she left home to work as household help. I know that she was very well liked. The last family that she worked for moved to Sault Ste. Marie and almost every summer they stopped by for a couple of days to visit us. This lady owned perhaps fifty buildings in the Sault and was very wealthy. She let us know, in many ways, that she had very warm feelings for my mother.

The Thom family, left to right, Lawrence, Hazel, Lena, Jim, Bella with Baby Meryle.

My dad worked in the mines and met my mother when she was 21. He was 33. I will never ever know what brought them together. My mother was a lady right down to her toes. Dad had a very dirty vocabulary, and had no qualms in using it. Every second word was an oath. I know he could hold his tongue when he wanted to, but he seldom was in the mood to want to. However, he must have really held back when he courted my mother. They were married April 10, 1901.

After a few months, they decided to move back home to the Spanish area where Dad's family now lived and were farming. Spanish was a small town at the mouth of the Spanish River, flowing into Georgian Bay.

They came from Parry Sound to Spanish by water (definitely not Mom's choice). She couldn't even look at water without being sick. By this time she was newly pregnant. Dad ate peaches and Mom felt sicker and sicker. It was fully twenty years before she could ever eat peaches again.

They moved in with Dad's family until Dad could build a home on the 160 acres that he owned just one mile south of his parents. Two months after they left Parry Sound, Mom received the news of her mother's death. She had suffered several miscarriages and was not in good health. This was a tremendous blow to Mom. Luckily her mother-in-law was very kind to her. They had very warm feelings for each other. Grandma Thom was the only doctor for many miles around. She delivered all of our family except the youngest. Mom was several months pregnant when Grandma was dying. Almost her last words were to Mom regretting that she wouldn't be around to deliver this last one. Mom's first son was Lawrence born February 14, 1902. What a great Valentine!

The house my parents built was very small. Money was almost non-existent. Once they had five children, they decided they could build an addition to the home. They added two rooms, one up and one down.

Very happily they moved into the new addition on Saturday; now at last they would have the space Mom had badly needed for a long time. On Sunday evening, as they were eating their evening meal, they smelled smoke and realized the house was on fire. They lost everything except for a few things from the kitchen. We have no pictures or material things from before that time.

Verna's mother and father, Bella (Fisher) Thom and Jim Thom, on their 50th Anniversary in 1951.

Mom had a badly sprained wrist at the time of the fire and so wasn't wearing her wedding ring. On their fiftieth anniversary, Dad bought her a diamond and a wedding ring. During all the years while rearing a family in a very strict community Mom wore no wedding ring. Everyone knew the story, but I am sure it must have crossed her mind many times to regret the lack of a ring. She never mentioned it, knowing that as long as there were children to raise, there was never the money.

Just across the road from us was an abandoned house belonging to a relative. My parents were given permission to use it until they could build another. Dad went right ahead and got started on the new one. The neighbours were marvellous, as usual. They brought pots, pans, quilts, furniture, and anything they could spare. When anyone started feeling sorry for her, Mom always answered that it could have been worse. They all came out alive. If ever she felt sorry for herself, no one knew it. She had a very strong character. She looked ahead and got on with her life. There was always something else to be done.

Verna's nephews, Colin Streich and Carl Meierhoff beside the home where she grew up.

Our mother was so very strict with our table manners that we would have rebelled if we had dared. Of course behind her back we called her Nag, Grouch, etc. In later years we really blessed her. We had the best manners of all our peers! We told her many times in our later years that we really appreciated the old Nag.

Mom could hitch up a team of horses and drive them, or take a man's place in the field. She was a beautiful housekeeper and a terrific cook. Most people are capable of cooking a delightful meal when surrounded by the latest gadgets and anything they might fancy from the store. Mom started from scratch; no fancy mixers or food. She just took the basics and used what she had and each time came up with something scrumptious. Her four daughters followed in her footsteps and were all good cooks, but each of us had a little more to work with. No matter how slim the materials on hand, she could always come up with a variety of interesting dishes. We never felt that we were poor. Is this why my youngest brother became a cook in

A neighbour offered Verna's mother a drive to town.

World War II and went on to have his own bakeshop? My only granddaughter is a dietitian. She is also a terrific cook. She and I have been exchanging recipes since she was ten.

Dad used to work in the lumber camp all winter. Jobs were very scarce and this provided the much-needed cash. The older children who were able worked at any job available. Mom was left with only very small children to help. She had stock to look after, cows to milk, chickens and pigs to feed, wood to bring in and many more jobs to do. The team of horses went with Dad to the camp, so supplies had to be brought home from the store by hand sleigh or a kind neighbour.

One year Mom fell out of the loft while putting hay out for the stock. There were no x-rays and Grandma Thom did the best she could, but Mom walked with a slightly crooked leg for the rest of her life. This injury never kept her away from her duties. All the time she was healing, she kept on working with her leg in a splint.

When evening came and chores were done, we sat around the room, each doing something. The children had homework, but when it was finished we found something else to do. Mom hooked rugs, made quilts, and made our clothing. Wool from our sheep was sent to the mills to be made into yarn. We kids wound the woollen skeins into balls, and what competition we had each trying to get his or hers wound first. Of course just when you thought you might come out the winner, your yarn tangled and held you back.

At this time I learned to knit. We girls had our choice of mending, darning socks, or knitting. That is when I acquired a love for knitting, for who wouldn't knit when the alternative was darning socks! (I am not a great mender).

The week started off on Monday with the washing. There was also bread to bake. Sunday there was usually company so by Monday we would be short of bread. On Tuesday there was ironing and churning. Wednesday was a real catch up day. Every day there was usually a cake or biscuits to bake, but on Wednesday an abundance of baking took place; things like pies and cookies that would keep. On Thursday or Friday we churned again and did some of the long range cleaning and another batch of bread. On Saturday the house was cleaned from top to bottom and baking was done again for Sunday and the company we took for granted. Our home was always open house for anyone dropping in, invited or otherwise.

There were also the seasonal jobs. In the fall at hog killing time, we made sausage (we cleaned our own casings), lard was rendered and headcheese was made. In the winter, Mom always had a quilt and hand hooked rugs on the go. She made all the girls' clothing plus the men's work shirts. There was a never-ending amount of mending, patching and darning. Much of this was done in the evening when we were "resting".

We always had a large garden, which was considered women's work. The men would plough it, and perhaps help plant it, but the weeding and use of it was always the women's job.

Mom always had beautiful flowers. The sweet peas and other fragrant flowers were always there to attract the bees and humming birds. Flowers grew up by the windows and many times we stood at the windows and could almost touch the humming birds. I have only once seen a humming bird since I left home. Humming birds, when I think of them, are always associated with my growing years.

Whenever there was illness in a family, or an accident, Mom was always right there to help. She was one of the very best in cases of sickness. Nothing put her off. She would have made a great nurse or doctor. The oldest girl, Lena, was just the same. Both must have been inspired by my Grandma Thom. Mom had some pretty grim jobs to do, but never backed off from any of them. She was more than cool in a crisis, and never seemed to get flustered.

One of the most vivid memories that comes to mind is when a neighbour had an accident in the field next to us. He was mowing hay with the old horse drawn mower. He stopped the horses and stepped in front of the blades to clear them out. The mower was in gear, which was a "no no". The horses stepped ahead for a tempting bit of grass and Nick had his leg cut right to the bone in the deepest part of the calf. My brother Jack heard him calling for help. Mom, Dad and Jack went to help. We phoned for the doctor and other help. There was at that time no hospital closer than Sudbury, about seventy miles away, so we automatically stayed at home unless it was surgery or something requiring special needs. When they brought Nick into the house, his wife looked at him and quietly dropped to the floor in a dead faint. Frances had never had any children, so she wasn't used to any first aid jobs. Mom was the doctor's aid that day. During the whole of his recovery, Mom did the nursing.

At the time of the accident, our whole family was preparing to go blueberry picking. Ten minutes later and there would have been no one home at our place. There were no other close neighbours to the field where he was working.

My mother firmly believed in God. She also believed in helping wherever there was a need. (Is this where we evolved into our volunteer jobs?) She went to church when it was possible and made sure that we went also. She helped wherever she was needed.

Our day began with the outside chores. As children, we milked the cows and then brought the milk to the house to run it through the separator. The skim milk was then taken back out to the calves and pigs. The hens had to be fed and water set out for them. In summer, we hurried through our household chores and then it was out to the fields to weed the fields of turnips, potatoes or the garden. We also did all the berry picking. We helped with the hay and harvest. When a load of hay was dumped in the haymow, we had to have it spread before the next load came in. We were supposed to tramp it down as much as we could. Our favourite way of packing it was to get up on the beams and jump onto the loose hay which had just been dumped there. That hay was really well packed!

In 1925 Lena, the oldest girl, was married. The next summer Larry, the oldest in the family, was married. Depression caught us just as we had been getting on our feet a little. We had managed to add on to the tiny house we were living in. Soon all of the others married and all had families except Lena. She mothered not only our whole family, but everyone else she knew. All of the family, except me, lived from Sudbury to the Soo. There were seventeen

Bella (Fisher) Thom, third from the left with three of her sisters: Winnie, Almira, and May.

grandchildren. I never did count up how many great grandchildren, but Mom knew them all plus their ages, names, and birthdays.

When I was nineteen, our lives were drastically changed by the death of our sister Hazel. She was very much loved by us all. She and Lena, after working away, had bought many things for us that we never ever would have had otherwise. She had a devilish sense of humour; not the kind that hurts anyone, but one that everyone could enjoy.

Hazel had been married a year and she was expecting her first baby. Unfortunately, she had had Scarlet Fever when she was in her teens. This left her kidneys badly damaged. My mother stayed with her for two weeks while she lay dying. What strength it must have taken to be there and be so helpless. This was just before the discovery of Sulfa and Penicillin.

She brought Carl Meierhoff, Jr., home to us and we kept him until he was six. He then spent school years in the Soo with his Dad and other grandparents, and came to us for the summers.

Mom spent a lot of time with each of her children, as she was needed. She came to each of us when we had our children or had sickness. She also saw her sister through a bout of cancer. She had diabetes in a mild form but took gangrene in her foot. She had her foot removed when she was eighty- five. We were all quite relieved when she recovered from it nicely. She lived another year and finally succumbed to cancer the next year.

Through all her years she showed her strength and instilled her morals to her family. She never complained. Her mind remained clear and lucid. Right to the end she could talk world affairs or anything else that came up. Her eighty-six years were well spent and well remembered by her family.

QUILTING AND RUG MAKING

In the winter, the ladies of the community always had, at the very least, one quilt ready for quilting. Five other ladies were invited to come for the day. Only good quilters were asked and Mom was considered to be very good. They chatted and sewed, and caught up on news. Quite a few quilts were made and a fair amount of visiting done. They came in the morning and could complete a quilt in a day. When it was our turn, Mom and I would have the quilt in the frames the night before ready for the visitors the next day. I would cook the meals and do the general work while the quilting was going on. I could quilt but didn't like doing it.

These were the opportunities to exchange new quilt patterns. Very few had access to magazines or pattern books. Their patterns were handed down from relatives and friends. Sometimes a visiting relative from a distance could bring some new and beautiful ones. They also managed to take back with them some of our cherished ones. Most families had one or more daughters near marriageable age. These daughters usually had several quilts in their hope chests by the time they were married.

One day another lady offered her services at the quilting bee. Mom had seen her quilting before and it looked excellent. She wasn't one of the regulars and lived a little farther away. In the evening when everyone had gone home, Mom and I took the quilt out of the frames, and she commented on the nice even stitches this lady had made. She shook the quilt out proudly, turned it over, and gazed in horror. The lady had left all her knots for everyone to see! They should have been pulled through inside the quilt. Mom and I spent every spare minute for the next few weeks making those knots disappear!

Store-bought clothes were rather rare; they had to be purchased from the Eaton's or Simpson's catalogues. But mostly it was yard goods that we purchased from the catalogue. These lengths of cloth were then made into our main garments and all those beautiful remnants and pieces of material were just waiting to become a part of those gorgeous quilts!

When our friends came to visit, we loved to reminisce. Which of us has had a dress from this material, or an unusually nice apron from this one. This was from a piece of goods that was given to us but had not quite enough material for a garment. It ended up making itself known in some of the quilt blocks. Quilts in those days were always what we called "pieced quilts". Later, over the years, they were embroidered and put together with plain blocks. Of course this kind of quilt was made much more quickly; none of the beautiful matching and piecing of the authentic pieced quilt. My favourite was the Log Cabin. Even with this standard one, there were various patterns, and they were all different and beautiful.

Then there was the old utility quilt that was not brought to anyone's attention. This was strictly for warmth and not for style. It was made of anything warm that could be put together. The boys of the family loved this type, as it was dark and more liveable. It would readily stand up to the romping and wrestling of my brothers, and was also warm. Old coats were ripped apart, and the better parts used, as were women's skirts. This material was put together in just any form, (crazy quilting) and stitched down on an old sheet – flannelette, cotton, or even dyed sugar bags. If you wanted to put a little jazz into it, you might do a brightly coloured herringbone stitch at all of the seams. This did make it much easier to look at. No wonder it was called a "crazy quilt". It was not dignified by having a quilting! It was "tied" every four inches or so with a double strand of colourful yarn. A crazy quilt could be tied in an afternoon by one person, but how warm and cosy these ugly old things were on a cold winter night! Many a romance started just from sharing one of those ugly old quilts when out driving. There was no worry that we might ruin them.

We had only wood fires, which were usually dead by morning. We always wakened up seeing our breath, but still those old ugly quilts had kept us snug as a bug in a rug.

Mom also hooked rugs. These were made from a burlap base, and our old woven woollen clothes were cut in very fine strips and hooked. Most of them were dyed in brilliant colours for contrast. One very good source was the old long john underwear.

Every winter there was a rug-hooking bee for the ladies of the neighbourhood. By the time each lady had given a quilt bee and a rug bee, they had their social life caught up. There was always a demand for braided rugs. These were the lowest down on the scale of rug making. Anything at all could be utilized for these. I still love hooked rugs. I never think of them as being ugly. To me they were "pioneer make do" at its very best. What a difference, stepping out onto a nice cozy rag rug or a cold bare floor! No matter how poor you were, you could always afford a rag rug, for it could be made from actual rags.

One day when I was at Black Creek Village, one of the ladies showed me several shortcut ways to make them. These required no sewing. I have made a few since then and I always appreciate her sharing the short cut ways to rag rug making.

MAKING DO

Our family consisted of eight children. I am quite positive that my mother used almost every invented short cut, plus a few she invented herself. We were very poor, often ill clothed, but very clean and never hungry or cold. I can remember a hard working childhood but a happy one.

When an animal was butchered, nothing was wasted. We made headcheese and sausage from the pork. We cleaned our own casings. Now I walk by the cleaned casings in the butcher shop and shudder to think of those horrible hours spent at such a despised job. However, the end result, the sausage, was worth every bit of it. I have never been able to buy anything that came close to the mouth-watering sausages my mom turned out. They were flavoured with a touch of sage and other seasonings. Perhaps this is just nostalgia, although I don't think so.

At Sugar Lake – Bella Thom with grandchildren Colin, Carl, Elwyn Byers (a friend), Marvin, Aldene, and Baby Audrey in front.

We did not use the blood, but a German neighbour always came and collected it. He took it home and made blood sausage. We used the liver, heart, kidneys, and tongue. Pig's knuckles and sauerkraut is still one of my favourite meals and I cook it several times a year. The lard was rendered and used for cooking. Pies were made from the rendered lard as long as we had it. My brothers used the bladder. They blew it up with an old pipe stem and used it as a football.

Headcheese was another favourite. We always looked forward to it. My father-in-law loved my headcheese. He said that anyone who could make that kind of treat should make the whole pork into headcheese.

For summer use, the meat was pickled in a brine heavy with salt, brown sugar, and pepper; a little saltpetre was added to change the meat from a dull grey to a lovely pink colour. Sometimes some molasses was added for flavour. Any fats not consumed were saved and later, when enough had accumulated, soap was made from it. I loved this soap, as the tallow in it made your hands quite soft. I myself made it during the war when there was never enough soap.

Verna's sister, Lena Stinson, and their dad. These fish, ready for smoking, were caught at Cutler Lake.

In the summer when we were lucky enough to have game or beef, we canned it in large two-quart jars. We made a great stock from the bones and canned that also. Fish were always there and easy to procure. We had no hydro and no refrigeration. Our non-laying hens were also canned in the same manner. I can still remember those dumplings Mom used to make for us. This also stretched the meat. For a stew she would take about a pound of meat, or some of the canned chicken, and with all of the additional vegetables, gravy, and dumplings, it turned into the most salivating meal for eight people. It was made in a large round flat pan that must have held at least six or seven quarts. I have never, even in the antique markets, seen a pan of that size or dimensions. I haven't a clue as to where Mother ever found it. This pan also baked our beans and many of the other goodies she made for us.

In the fall, eggs were packed in a substance called water glass, which preserved them for some time. We grew our own veggies and dried beans. And of course, being on the farm, there was always plenty of milk. We loved the cottage cheese. Milk was used to make beautiful puddings, rice, custard, trifle, chocolate, and many other dishes.

I learned many cooking skills from my mother. There was always a large pot of soup on the stove. We were allowed, when we came in from the cold, to have a bowl of the nice thick vegetable soup. We made our own pasta, also our bread. I must have been about eight or nine the first time I ever saw a loaf from the bakery. It was also one of the first things I learned to bake.

We would have about twice a week, in the winter, a great pot of baked beans. This was great protein for us and replaced meat. The seven or eight of us could make those beans disappear in a hurry. We also cooked dried peas as a source of protein. Of course we hadn't heard about proteins then; but we did know they were very tasty and filling. Mom could take a small amount of meat and a great amount of veggies and make the most temptingly tantalizing meat pie; it was easy to forget that there was only a little meat in it. After I was married, this was my husband's favourite meal. I used up the end of a roast, plus a week's supply of leftovers, gravy and veggies. This was topped with a biscuit topping. We had no salads, but when vegetables were being prepared we consumed vast quantities of raw ones.

In the winter, my dad and brothers cut ice and saved it in an ice- house, covered with loads of sawdust. In the early years we didn't have this. When I was in my early teens, my sisters, who were working out, gave us the idea of the ice, besides furnishing us with an ice-box. This was small but a real miracle to us who had never had anything like it before. There were only a few of the neighbours who put up ice. It was much later that this caught on and more people took advantage of the free cooling system.

New clothing was very rare. It of course went to the older ones. We younger ones received the hand-me-downs to be made over for us. We also received used clothing from some cousins who were older and more affluent. One unforgettable time in my life was when for two weeks, I must wear my brother's shoes. As soon as money came in I had new ones, but I could not, for a long time forget the embarrassment it caused me.

Verna's brother-in-law, Bernie Streich, with a 22 pound trout caught in Lake Temiskaming at Kippewa, Quebec, where he was based while a section foreman for C.P.R.

Our flour and sugar came in 98 pound bags, and in a year's time, we accumulated quite a few; however, there was never nearly enough. Flour bags had a coarser weave, but was a little (comparatively) softer. Sugar bags had a very firm and harder weave.

Our underpants and slips were made of flour bags, as were our nighties and aprons. The aprons were often dyed and embroidered quite beautifully. The sheets were flour bags and the pillowcases were of sugar bags. Pillow cases mostly included a border or insert of hand crocheted lace. The dish towels were flour bags. Flour bags also lined a quilt if it wasn't a real special one. Trousseau quilts had fine cotton linings ordered specially from the catalogues.

The lettering on these bags was set with a very good quality dye. Flour bags were much easier to bleach than sugar bags. Always somewhere on an article you might read "Redpath" in large red letters or "sweeten it" in black in smaller letters. These words often crept into your undergarments because they could be covered up with your outer clothes. Imagine playing in the school yard when an errant wind could invite someone to "sweeten it"!

We always had sheep. Our wool was sent to the factory to be manufactured into yarn. We knit sweaters, scarves, knee length socks, toques and mittens from this. It took a terrific amount of yarn to keep a large family clothed and warm. I remember large sacks of wool being picked up at the station. It was called wheeling yarn and was grey or white. It came in either two or three strands.

When the sock feet wore out after much darning, we cut off the feet and knit new ones. The legs would wear out three pair of feet. Old sweaters were salvaged of their better parts. This yarn was used for scarves and toques as they didn't need a strong yarn to be warm. It was also used for darning or added to a new strand to make a slightly bulkier sweater.

My dad and brothers spent every moment they weren't doing other jobs in keeping an inexhaustible supply of firewood for us. We sold cords of it whenever we could find a customer.

Jeanette Thibeau, a friend, with Verna's son Warren Thaxter (6 years) and her daughter Marilyn (2 years) 1951. Wherever they lived Jim felt more comfortable with a large supply of wood.

Luckily, my dad was an excellent carpenter as well as a farmer. Wood was cheap and he made the most of it. He made most of our furniture, as well as our playthings. He made Mom's knitting needles, quilting frames, wooden kitchen utensils, bowls, toys, and just about anything that could be made from wood.

Nothing was wasted. Ropes were spliced. Harness was patched until there was almost none of the original left. We had a couple of shoe makers' lasts; our shoes were patched, soles and heels added from old leather.

Anyone who took us out for a sleigh ride, always furnished us with plenty of buffalo robes and those crazy quilts. These were placed over a bed of hay and it was a lover's dream to snuggle down with your boy friend or fiancé.

There was usually an open-air rink for skating and hockey games, but we also used a creek or lake, or whatever was handy. When we arrived home Mom would often have, as a special treat, a large pot of hot chocolate for us.

The nearest village had only about one hundred people. We had no theatre or bowling alley, but then we couldn't have afforded it if there had been. We did have a Community Hall. When a couple married they gave a dance in the hall. I have many great memories of those dances.

In our family, we were very lucky that my dad was such a great handyman. He made many pieces of our furniture. I would like to have had him around after we were married. It was war time. I, like most of my peers, had orange crate and butter box furniture for many years. They made end tables, nightstands, and cupboards for dishes and groceries; were used for storage chests, footstools, toy boxes, and food carriers and just about anything you might imagine.

The early training I received has followed me all through the years. Being poor does not mean that meals have to be monotonous. There is plenty of variety even in cheap food if you have the initiative to try. I never throw away anything that can be used and recycled. The word "recycle" was never used but it was our very survival during the depression. I cannot, to this day, diaper a baby with paper diapers, without thinking of the lovely soft cotton ones to which our children were accustomed. The diapers were small size at first, then larger, and finally near training time, a small one used inside the larger one. When toilet training was completed, the diapers were packed away ready for the next one. When they became too thin to use, their usefulness was not over. There was many a child's tears wiped away with a threadbare diaper. They were great dusters and they out-shone any paper towel I have ever used in clean up jobs. Sometimes, but not always, "the old is best".

Verna's son Warren (5 years) and daughter Marilyn (1 year), 1949.

HAIR

Mother was our barber. She lined us up one after the other to be shorn like a lamb at shearing time. Her only source of tools was the very unbarberlike comb and a pair of household scissors. The boys had the typical “bowl” hair cut. We girls had ours cut quite short, parted in the middle and bangs. Every child in school had an identical haircut, except for two German girls who had long hair. In our school we didn’t dare have long hair! We had two families with a permanent case of “cooties” so, no matter how we tried to escape, we very often came home scratching. We dreaded what we knew what was in store for us.

Those two families who periodically gave us head lice, gave Mom horrors, and she consequently gave us the dousing of our lives, darned near taking the skin off our heads. All the while she lectured us about sitting with these kids. We tried but we liked them and they liked us. We also felt sorry for them. We often brought these little trouble making creatures home with us through no fault of our own. There were never quite enough clothes hooks to go around at school and often when they were last in, they would hang their clothes over ours and the damage was done. At home, Mom would see some of us scratch and her suspicions were aroused. We knew that we were all in for a horror night. She put pure coal oil, (kerosene) on our hair and then used a fine comb, over and over. We were then bathed and our clothes were washed and boiled. We used to hate Mother those times, but later I understood.

I had very straight hair and if the fairy godmother had granted me one wish, I would have asked for curly hair. Most of my family had curly hair and I thought it just wasn’t fair, especially as the boys resented the curls they possessed and were always trying to straighten them out.

I was seventh child in a family of eight so I didn’t get much attention. My younger brother was born when I was five and a half, and my older sister came home to help Mom for a month. Lena was a dearly beloved sister twelve years my senior. In my whole life I have never met anyone who was so dear and well loved. This was just not my own opinion, but everyone else, to the end of her life, felt as I did. While Lena was home helping, I knew she had her hands full and I never asked for favours. But Lena was one of those people who knew just what you wanted without asking. The first Saturday night she was there, she took me on her knee; “Vern,” she said, “how would you like to have a nice head of curly hair tomorrow?” Wow! This was Christmas, Birthday, and Fairy Godmother all rolled into one! That evening, and every Saturday evening while she was at home, she put my hair up in rags, our only hair curlers of the time. Never in this world was anyone so proud as that first Sunday I had beautiful auburn curls all over my head!

This seemed to satisfy my longing for curly hair. Even though I still liked curly hair, the desperate wanting was no longer there, but I never forgot the suspense of walking in to show the family my curls.

One hair cutting evening, when I was about seven or eight, Mom started on the job. Lena was home for overnight and asked if she might help. I offered myself to her. She started on my hair and couldn't get it quite right. She kept on trimming here, on this side and balancing it on the other side, until finally she stepped back and gave me a long over all look. She had a horrified look on her face. My hair at the back was cut short almost up to the crown of my head. She looked as if she were about to cry, but I threw my arms around her and assured her I loved it. I know I was teased a bit about it at school but it didn't bother me because my beloved sister had done it.

Lena and my next sister, Hazel, were the cause of a slight family rift between my parents. This was in the early twenties. The girls worked just twenty miles away and sometimes had Mom visit them overnight. Once when Mom came home from Webbwood, she entered the house and took off her hat. Dad just about exploded! She had a short hair cut! Only women of loose morals did that, and he wasn't going to have a wife with that kind of reputation!

Dad's vocabulary was not quite as clean as mine. But as he couldn't do a darn thing about it, he soon cooled down. It suited Mom, as she had very fine hair, and not too much of it. Her hair pins were always falling out.

My mother lived to be 86 and I can hardly remember a time when her hair was not just as neat as a pin, and for the last 50 years, snow white. Even when she was bed ridden near the last, the hairdresser came in regularly to do her hair.

I loved to play with Mom's switch and hairpieces because they were the exact same auburn as mine. Mom, however, didn't like it and I grew up with the idea that red hair was not nice. That was something else that belonged with loose morals. I think she was very pleased when her auburn turned grey. Later, after I left home, I discovered that auburn was not so bad. I easily answered to 'Red'.

A real event in my life was when I was in my late teens and earned enough money to buy my first perm, but it never quite lived up to that first head of curls created by my sister.

FOOD

My mother was a great cook. She could take the very plainest fare of old country cooking, but with special touches it became just that little extra, even using potatoes, flour and common every day items.

I remember she would take mashed potatoes, milk, just a wee bit of flour, and baking powder, and make a dough. This was rolled out and cooked in the frying pans. They looked like pancakes but were so very different. We put butter, syrup or jam on these and they were absolutely mouth-watering.

No matter how poor we were, we always had a Christmas cake and pudding. Mom began early in the fall buying an item at a time until she had the ingredients for this much-longed-for treat. It was the only time of year that we had anything so expensive. Even the eggs were hoarded. We might do without eggs most of the winter, but she always made sure she had enough for these two important items. Hens, in those days, didn't know they were supposed to lay all winter. If perhaps we had coaxed them along with expensive feed and catered to them, they might have reconsidered. But we didn't have the feed, the money, or the know-how and the hens quit laying in October. Mom started early putting the eggs in water glass. A large wooden pail or small tub was used. A can of water glass (a jelly like substance) was emptied into the vessel, then water was added. This coated the eggs and kept them for many months.

It was no easy task to prepare the fruit and nuts. The walnuts had to be cracked (we had not at that time heard of almonds); the peel, which came in large chunks, had to be cut up finely; as did the dates. The large Muscat raisins had not only to be chopped but seeded as well.

It must have been a sacrifice to have the eggs go to the storage rather than to the store, as this was one of our main bartering items that bought the other items that were so necessary – such as sugar, flour, tea, coal oil, and many other essentials.

The eggs didn't taste especially nice after storage, but were perfect for cooking. Mom knew she had to have eggs for the Christmas cake and pudding or they would never turn out right – that is until the year when she had her cakes in the oven about half an hour and discovered the eight eggs still in the bowl on the table. They were put back in storage. It was one time Mom had a really red face. The cakes were delicious but were sort of crumbly when sliced.

A few special pieces of hardwood for baking her cake were put aside until the great day came. The wood oven had to be kept at a very low heat for quite awhile, and the hardwood was ideal for this as it never flared up and became too hot. One day Dad came in when Mom was out for just five minutes or so, decided the house was freezing, and piled quick heat burning wood in the stove. Mom came back just in time to rake it out and save her cakes. The wood fire was not the only thing that flared that day!

I am not too fond of cottage cheese unless it is dressed up with other items. The cottage cheese we used to make was not even a distant relative of the modern day cottage cheese. In the morning, a large soup pot was filled with milk and set on the back of the stove, just on the edge of the reservoir. It kept just about lukewarm until evening when it had separated from the whey. It was drained and put in cheesecloth and hung up to drip overnight. In the morning if there was any moisture left in, it was squeezed out. It was then emptied into a bowl, and salt and pepper were added making the most delicious bowl of crumbly cheese. You could take it in your hand and eat it, that is, if your mother didn't catch you. If it was pressed, it was like regular cheese.

Every week we churned the week's supply of cream. That was a job I heartily disliked. The churn, butter bowl, and all the utensils had to be scalded and then cooled down with cold water. When the butter was churned there were pails and pails of cold water fresh from the pump to bring in. The buttermilk was drained from the butter and then the butter had to be washed many times until the water came off clear. Salt was added and probably a bit of carotene for colouring. Mostly the colouring was added to the cream, but if it was missed it could be added to the butter. In the summer time when the cows were on grass, the butter didn't need any colouring, but for the rest of the year it was too pale and colour had to be worked into the butter, because it would be streaky looking if not worked enough. All in all, it took about ten pails of water from the scalding of utensils until everything was washed up.

The buttermilk was a bonus. We grew up on buttermilk. I could drink it several times a day. We used it for pancakes, biscuits, cake, and many other things. It gave them a flavour that has no comparison. The modern buttermilk, so I am led to believe, is just sweet milk and baking powder left at a certain temperature.

When we were in the fields working, there was always both buttermilk and cold water. This must be part of the reason that we were so strong and healthy. I think we had the germs so scared that they didn't dare come near us. We certainly never heard of a germ until we were grown up. They must have been in hiding until we started eating fast foods and all the other not-so-good foods we used later.

We always had a large vegetable garden. We also had a large crop of turnips and potatoes. We could use about 50 pounds of potatoes in a week with just our own family. In those days a bag of potatoes was a back-breaking 100 pounds. This was also one of our few cash crops; that is if we could find someone with money to buy them. We also used the barter system. One year my brother spent a few days ploughing for a neighbour who had been ill. Of course there was never any question of being paid, we were used to helping out as help was needed. A week later, the neighbour arrived bringing three large bags of cabbage and a bag of onions. Our crop of both had not done well and this was his way of saying "Thank you".

Dad planted as few onions as he could get away with as he didn't like them and saw to it that Mom didn't put them in his food. A couple of my brothers followed suit and wouldn't touch them. The rest of us were onion starved. On days when Dad was away, we went onion crazy. We put onions in everything and fried up a large pan full to satisfy our cravings. I swore I would never marry a man who didn't like onions. Well, the man I married did like them, but it back-fired on me a bit when I found that his favourite bed time snack was a peanut butter and onion sandwich. Oh well, sometimes you just can't win!

We very often seemed to have someone else at meal times. If anyone dropped in near mealtime in the country, it was taken for granted that he or she would stay and eat with us. This was a bonus for the bachelors and widowers in the area, and my mother had a reputation as an excellent cook.

When potato planting came around, the potato seed was cut the night before. Next morning we were all out ready for the planting, which was done by hand. Even if it was not a school holiday, we stayed home for that. Pupils were scarce in the school house for a day or so. Bags of seed were left at the top of the rows, where we filled our pails, then came the tedious job of dropping them the required distance in the rows that the plough had made. Each farmer had his own idea of how far apart the seeds should be planted. In any case, it didn't seem to matter, because if it was a fair year, everyone had a good crop, even the farmers who were told they had planted at the wrong time of the moon.

When our potatoes were planted, that didn't mean that we were finished. Dad lent us out to our uncle and then to two other neighbours who had no kids.

Turnip gathering was a nasty job, as the weather usually was cold and wet. Turnips were slow growers and didn't do much until the first frost, and then they grew like magic. They were left until late to harvest as they seemed to keep on growing forever. Because it was late, we often pulled them in snow. We went down between a couple of rows and worked each row. They had to be pulled and the earth loosened from them. The roots and tops were trimmed with a sharp knife and the turnips were then left in rows to be thrown into the wagon later. The tops were saved for a treat for the cows. Special care had to be taken not to give them too much at a time as it made the milk and cream taste bitter. The larger turnips were strong and stubborn. When we were small, we sometimes had to have a little help to pull the larger ones. We were never too small or too young to work in the fields.

Potato picking time was in September. They were ploughed out very gently and we went along with our buckets to gather the harvest. When we had a pail full we would help each other by one holding the bag while the other emptied our containers. Of course where there are kids, there is always a little horseplay, but after getting a hiding, we managed to behave ourselves.

This was real back breaking work. We would be out in the fields by 8:30 and except for an hour at noon, we were at it until about 5:00. Chores had to be done at both ends of the day, and the next day we were at it again. We had a fairly large crop, as we needed so many for our own use and it was always a much needed cash item if we could find a buyer or two.

Potato harvesting, our own and the time spent with our neighbours, lasted about ten days. We had never heard of coffee breaks. We always had a pail of water for drinking or a pail of buttermilk, but it was not even a proper pit stop, for as soon as we had our drink, it was back to the spuds. We had only a few short weeks before our turnip crop had to be harvested.

If we harvested the turnips in the snow, we used gloves or mitts, but they were saturated almost as soon as we started. Sometimes it was a hard frost but just as cold. The turnips had to be brought into the stable where a special bin was ready to receive them. There was a supply brought to the cellar at the house for our use. And of course when our own crop was in, it was off to the neighbours again to do theirs. We used to be at this until late in October. We have worked at pulling turnips all day and gone out for Hallowe'en in the evening.

When we were fortunate in having a deer or moose, we had to can it in jars. We always gave a large quantity away. Other neighbours did the same for us when they had fresh meat. The men in our family were all excellent shots.

We had a large number of bones left after canning. They were boiled down and made the most delectable soup. We concentrated some and canned that also. Mom made her own noodles. They were made with eggs and flour and rolled out thin. She would put clean towels over the chair backs and put a large sheet of them to dry for an hour or so, then cut them in strips to be put into the soup. I drool when I think of this soup. No wonder I never lost my taste for homemade soup. By summer most of the fruit jars were empty of their former contents and we were only too happy to see them full to the brim of the goodness of nature.

Canning and pickling started in June with the wild strawberries and continued until late fall. After the strawberries, came the blueberries in very plentiful supply, then the raspberries, quite plentiful but more time consuming to harvest. We made pin cherry, choke cherry and apple jelly, and many different jams. We had the wild fruit to can and some of us were lucky enough to have a few fruit trees at home. At that time very few people had gone in for fruit trees. Everyone thought the seasons were too cold. That was not so. They just had not tried the hardier types. We had a couple of plum trees and some apples. They weren't good eating apples but they cooked up well, as did the crab apples. It was always easy to procure a supply of cranberries to keep over the winter. Mother Nature was very good to us and in many cases kept us from many more hardships.

NATURE'S BOUNTY

Where would we have been without nature's bounty? Times were hard all over. It was depression time. No one had money to buy anything. Our farm was 160 acres with only about forty acres tilled. There were six or seven of us, mostly adults with no jobs for anyone. If you had decided to keep a beef for next winter's meat, it sounded good, but if by a miracle you had a chance to sell it, you jumped at the chance – even if it were only about five cents per pound. Perhaps it would sell "on the hoof" which meant the weight might be underestimated and you were the loser, take it or leave it. Mostly we took it and we looked elsewhere for our meat.

When we saw a deer in our fields, it stood little chance against the crack marksmen in our family. It was then shared with our neighbours. If it was summer, we canned it. Oh how good that tasted! The meat was sliced and put into two-quart jars. After cooling, the jars were lined up in the basement. This was sliced meat, with about an inch of jelled broth. Each jar contained pure meat with a teaspoon of salt and was then sealed and processed. We eagerly anticipated the mouth-watering casseroles and stews that would be made from them. And as a bonus, we had all those bones to make big pots of delicious soup.

In the fall we could hunt partridge, and this was the legal season for hunting deer and moose. A deer licence was $1.00 and a moose licence was $4.00. The season ran from November 1 to November 25. Our men usually went to a hunting camp for a few days, secured their limit and came home. Game was quite plentiful at that time. The hunting camp was a highlight in their life. It was their annual vacation. Not so for the women left behind. They had to do a week's baking and cooking ahead to supply the men in camp. Then they had all the chores and men's duties to attend to at home. Somehow or other the women never got around to having a vacation of their own.

I remember one summer that was extremely hard. We used on the average a hundred pounds of flour every three weeks. One hundred pounds of sugar lasted us six to eight weeks. More would be needed if wild fruit was plentiful. Then there was tea, coffee, coal oil for the lamps and lanterns, and many other things that had to be purchased. There was absolutely no cash to be had. Even though we were living on a farm, we had to sell anything that could be spared in order to purchase these urgent necessities. So an animal that we might have planned to use for ourselves was sold and we were left without protein.

For this reason, Dad, his brother and two neighbours decided to go moose hunting. A deer dressed only about 80 to 120 pounds, so a moose was what they set their sights on. (Sorry!)

They left early one morning, taking a team of horses and a boat. They went as far as they could go on an old logging road, where the team and wagon were then left. The men floated the boat and set out to find the moose. This beautiful country is dotted like a necklace with lakes, each running into the other, or connected with a small portage. In the late afternoon, they found their game and shot one large bull moose. After dressing him down, they found they could not fit the carcass and the four of them into the boat. After a bit of thought, they decided to remove all the bones of the carcass. This way they could, with gunwales at the water line, just make it float. There went our lovely soup bones!

But nature had a surprise for them! They had been so intent on making the cargo fit the boat, they hadn't noticed the weather. The wind was blowing a real gale, the white capped waves were smashing and pounding on the rocks making it impossible for them to navigate their boat across the lake. Nothing else for it, they would have to stay overnight. They had no camping equipment, but they gathered a supply of dry wood to get a fire going. It was now pouring rain and almost dark. Evergreen branches were cut and a wick-i-up was made to protect them from the downpour. With all that supply of fresh moose meat there was no question of going hungry.

Meanwhile back home Mother was having mental fits. She had a phobia of all things connected with bodies of water, so always expected the worst. In the morning she sent two of my brothers to find them. The wind and storm had abated during the night, and the sun was shining as the men made their way home about noon, to the relief of Mother and the other wives. How great that meat tasted to our protein starved bodies.

One favourite hunting story was of a sixteen-year-old lad who was out with his dad and a couple of other men. Mert had a .22; what he expected to do with it, other than shoot a couple of partridge, is neither here nor there. When an enormous bull moose in rut came roaring at him, Mert took to a tree and broke all records for climbing, but never for a moment did he think of abandoning his .22. That bull moose shook his antlered head, bellowed and tried to climb the tree too. Mert, in desperation, fired off a couple of his pea-shooter shots, and lo! and behold! by a lucky freak, hit a vulnerable spot. Needless to say he was the local hero of the teenagers (and the envy of the men) for years to come.

Note: The meat was so tough it was hardly fit to eat!

Partridge was very tasty. It was the one thing we rarely used out of season. During the fall, the men usually took a .22 with them when they brought the cows in from the bush. They usually managed to bring in several partridges as well.

Fish was always available. Our farm ran down to within a few yards of the Spanish River. There was a space from the farms to the river that was called the Broken Front and was owned by the teaching Sisters of a College at Spanish for Indian girls. We could walk down to the river any evening and catch a few fish. These varied, you might have as many as six different kinds of fish in an evening. Our gear consisted of a line with a hook. Near the hook, we had a bit of iron or lead for a sinker, and a cork a little higher for a float. We would step out on

Verna and her kid brother, Jim, showing off a muskie that their brother, Cliff, caught.

some large boom logs for a dock and throw in our lines. Sometimes we fished from a rock. We seldom arrived home empty handed.

In the spring, the suckers and smelts came up in the creeks to spawn. Everyone made a big deal out of netting these. Suckers were big and ugly, very coarse, and as far as I am concerned the less said about them the better. Well, it was the depression and plenty of people liked them. The smelts were usually netted at night, after the day's work was done. It was great sport for fishermen. They fished and visited in the light of the lanterns. Next day there were a bushel or two of smelt to be cleaned. Most of these were left to me to clean. Mother never let anything go to waste. She had a real knack for doing them up in different ways. Some were salted, others were pickled in mustard sauce. Just when the last of the smelts were cleaned, and my retching stomach had said "enough", the men went out and brought another lot home. It was not a bit of use saying "I've had it"; the parent's word was law, and I was only a kid. To this day I cannot eat a smelt or a strong tasting fish, rather I am very selective and eat only the mild tasting ones. I do, however, like seafood. It is nice that it was not plentiful where I grew up. Not ever having to clean it, I can enjoy it.

Earl Stinson holding fish that Jim Thom, Verna's dad, caught. On the right is Verna's brother-in-law, Ed Stinson. Woman and child are unknown.

Muskies were quite plentiful. My brother Cliff caught one that weighed in at 16 pounds. One Sunday at one of our family picnics, the men went fishing. My dad, thinking he had caught a log, started to haul it in and discovered he had hooked a 35-pounder. It almost filled the boat. I have pictures of both of these. The one I like the best, is the one that no one tried to catch, so of course he got away. There was a bay opening off the Spanish River with a small narrow inlet, about 25 feet wide by 150 feet long. The bay on the west side came up to the corner of our farm. The lake at the east end of the inlet was a favourite picnic place for everyone in the area. There were a number of family picnics there. One Sunday, my brother, Jack, was sunbathing on the steeply sloped rock that dropped down into the inlet, with just his toes in the water. He had a corn plaster on one toe. As he was idly wiggling his toe around, a big muskie snapped at it, and if Jack hadn't seen it a second before it snapped, he would have needed more than a corn plaster. About eight people saw it so this is not just another fish fable.

The fields and bushes gave up their bounties in season and were a most welcome addition to our limited larder. I suppose it would be fair to say, if you didn't grow it or find it in the woods, you didn't eat it. There certainly was no money for luxuries from the store.

First of the goodies was maple syrup time. We had a plentiful supply of hard maples on our farm. Dad made spiles from wood or pieces of pipe. A hole was bored into the tree and a spile was inserted. Our pails were left hanging on the spiles ready for the sap. Next morning we went round the tapped trees with a horse hitched to a jumper or sledge, and holding a large barrel for the sap. Some trees produced more sap than others. How good that sap tasted! Perfect weather for the sap was freezing cold nights and warm sunny days. We loved to get the sap gathering duties. The sun would be shining, and the first crows would be back telling us with their raucous cawing that spring was on its way. The snow was usually deep and if we were not too early in the day, it could generate a great snowball fight.

Sometimes the sap had a coating of ice on it, making it more flavourful. When we arrived home with the sap, a large fire was started to boil the sap down. If we had anything in plenty those days it was wood. It takes about eight gallons of sap to make 1 gallon of syrup. So it took some boiling down. Someone was always near it to keep the fire going. Splitting wood could always be done near it. When it began to get just a little syrupy, we would bring it into the house where Mother took over. It could go very rapidly from syrup to taffy, to sugar, to burning.

At the end of the season, we usually had a taffy pull. That was an event for us. We usually asked friends in for that evening. When the taffy was just at the perfect stage, we poured it over clean snow. If you were creative you could make fanciful shapes. When it was cool enough to handle, we started to pull it. If you had someone special, he helped you pull. It was a very sweet, messy, lovely time.

We made quite a supply of syrup. We also made sugar. We would have porridge in the mornings with thick cream and finely shaved maple sugar on it. I was never too fond of porridge because we had it every day, but with maple sugar, instead of the usual brown, it was special. I liked porridge after I left home and didn't have to eat it every day. But I take one percent milk and sweetener on it, a far cry from our early porridge days. My Scottish forebears would turn in their graves if they could see my breakfast bowl of porridge now.

Our next harvest came in late June and the first part of July. It was strawberry time. They were very tedious to pick, but we all loved them so much, we made a valiant effort to get as many as possible. There is nothing that compares with them in taste. Wild raspberries were at their best in August. These were very plentiful, and not as hard to pick as the strawberries.

Sometimes if we were lucky, we had a few blackberry bushes; never more than enough to make a couple of pies. Then there were pin cherries, very small but tasty. They were good only for jelly, but a very special jelly. Chokecherries were very plentiful, and still my very favourite jelly. They could be found along the fences and were very plentiful. They also made a terrific wine. The kitchen ceiling of our farm kitchen could testify to that, for the stains were still there when the house was torn down. This resulted from my two sisters not agreeing as to whether you should hold the bottle up and catch it coming back down or shoving the neck down into the large container. I think it was a tie.

Best of all were the blueberries, and also the best and easiest to harvest. They were also very sweet and took very little sugar. That in itself was a real bonus. I could write chapters on just blueberry stories. It was the one harvest you could always count on. They grew in lowlands and on the rocks. In a dry year, there were plenty in the lower land, but in a wet year, they grew better on the rocks in among the mosses. Everyone had blueberries – sometimes not in large quantities but if not, then one could walk or take the team of horses to some place within a mile or so. The younger fry picked close to home nearly every day. We had fresh blueberries and cream, or blueberry pie, every day. Another bonus was the quality of blueberries, which was unlike strawberries and raspberries – they could be kept for quite a few days.

The blueberry season coincided with the haying season. After a rain, when the hay had to dry for another day in the fields, we got down to serious blueberry picking. The horses were hitched to the wagon and the whole family, minus one, went to the most plentiful yielding places. The one left at home had to have supper ready for the rest of us. We set off in the morning with a picnic lunch. It is almost unimaginable how many berries five or six adults can pick in a day, and use in a year. We are speaking here of pails, baskets and sometimes even tubs. They were usually shared with anyone who was unable to go himself. There were also times when we didn't take the team, but just walked. Each one came home carrying two large pails. These became very heavy after the first mile. Blueberry weddings were quite common, usually followed by a blueberry infant some nine months later.

Cranberries were of two varieties. The high bush cranberries grew on trees, but were not as plentiful as the marsh ones. They were also valued for their keeping qualities. They would keep for some time as is, or could be frozen. These were a special treat in the winter. Frost to freeze them was not in short supply.

Wild mushrooms were plentiful and many people gathered them. At our house we were not allowed. At one time these were used, but after a family was poisoned, three children dying and another very ill, mushrooms were forbidden at our home. Quite understandable.

Hazelnuts grew and were lovely but any family with kids didn't harvest any, we had them all stripped off before they were ready. Sometimes a bee tree was found and we had a taste of wild honey.

A favourite place where raspberries were extra plentiful, was reached by going over rocks and bush for two or three miles. Twenty-five years later, my brother took me to this spot by car. There was not only a road into it, but it was a very popular area for summer homes.

Our farms were heavily wooded. There was never a shortage of wood. We had a mixture of softwood and hardwood. During the day, we used poplar, balm, and birch. During the night, we used the slower burning oak, maple and elm. Birch was also a good medium burning source of heat. We saved the hardwood to sell, as no one would buy the softwood. It also brought more money per cord.

Keeping warm in winter was a real challenge. Insulation was unknown, and there were drafts from every corner. We all gathered round the stoves. We had one stove going all year, but when late September came we looked forward to putting up the box stove or heater. The pipes had to be connected and we all crowded around for the first fire. Taking it down was another matter. In late April, when it came down, the pipes and chimney had to be cleaned. This was no small job. No matter how carefully you tried, soot managed to creep into the corners and over the furniture. It was ground into the floor. Taking down the stove was a despised chore and there was no use putting it off.

Our family always looked ahead. There were cords and cords of beautiful dried wood ready for the stoves at all times. The kitchen stove was used year round. In summer, the meals were cooked and water was heated on it. It gobbled up wood like Wimpy did hamburgers. It would be an astounding amount if ever we had counted up the number of cords used in our home during a year. Some families just barely kept ahead with their wood, and the women had to burn green wood. It was frustrating to keep a fire going with green wood. It caused a build up of carbon and soot in the chimneys that had to be cleaned out every six weeks or so. This was a terrible job, and had to be undertaken on a mild day. If neglected, it caused a chimney fire. We had one neighbour who just cut enough for a day at a time. Sometimes when he fell behind he drove to his dad's and brought home some dry wood to keep his home from freezing up. He drove his family crazy, as each day was a challenge to beat Jack Frost.

Some years ago when Verna visited the old place, she found they had named the roads. She couldn't resist taking this picture.

WASH DAY – BLUE MONDAY

Nothing is sure in this world except death and taxes, unless you lived in the country in the first half of the twentieth century; then you included the Monday morning wash.

No decent housewife could leave her clotheslines bare for all the neighbours to see and speculate; but what if it were raining? Too bad! That didn't leave you off the hook. It was not put off until Tuesday, because Tuesday had its own work. You just carried on. Perhaps the weather would break and you could hang out your clothes in the afternoon, still giving them time enough to dry. If it continued to rain, a few necessities were dried around the wood stove and the balance were ready to hang out whenever the weather was clear. A clothes dryer, in those days, was a lovely brisk wind.

The days of a housewife on a farm are very demanding. Each day has its own chores and tasks. There was ironing, churning, bread and other baking, cleaning, oil lamps to tend, gardening, milking, gathering eggs, and many more, making it essential that each day the daily tasks be carried out as usual or they could soon add up to an unwanted disaster.

The rain was not all bad. Huge rain barrels were always ready to receive the beautiful soft acid-free rain. Most of the wells in our area had very hard water full of lime and minerals. It was not easy to make good suds when washing. The rainwater, however, was soft and made suds to your elbows when using the scrub board. We always saved rainwater to wash our hair. Our hair acquired a sheen and softness that would rival any of the modern shampoos.

Washday actually started on Sunday evening. Water was pumped and carried in to fill the copper wash boiler, which had been placed on the back of the stove. It would be heating in the morning while breakfast and outside chores were being attended. It would then be brought forward to the front of the stove to get really hot. The cream separator and the dishes were always washed before the serious job of the day began. By this time the boiler was living up to its name.

Two tubs were placed on a bench. The rinsing tub was filled with water carried in from the well, and enough cold water to mix with the hot was placed in the wash tub. A scrub board was used. Everything was wrung by hand. It comes as no surprise that most country women in those days were strong armed and full busted. Three hours of scrubbing on a board with a bar of Comfort or P. & G. soap took care of that. In later years we bought an old hand wringer for 25 cents and thought we were in seventh heaven. It surely did save those over-worked wrist muscles.

The very delicate things had first attention, followed by white linens, and towels. Remember, coloured bedding was yet to come, and towels and linens were inevitably white. The whites were rinsed, put into the boiler for a good scalding, then rinsed again in a "blueing" water. Javex? Never heard of it! Dresses, aprons, and shirts were attended to next. These were now dipped into a starch mixture, which had been prepared the night before.

This was now the time for getting those first lines of clothes out, and glancing around to see who had or had not been first. Of course you could see only three or four homes, but the word would soon circulate via the party line telephone as to who had been first today. To be first was almost comparative to winning the Olympics.

Then back inside to finish the rest of the wash, mostly heavy working clothes. Used water was carried out and replaced several times, depending on the amount of washing to be done. There was usually not enough line room for all of the dark things, so they were put aside until the whites were dried. This was the time we wished for lots of strong breezes. The kitchen was tidied up and the floor got a quick wash.

A hot meal was then prepared and eaten by the family. If the weather was favourable, you could usually bring in the white clothes. Oh the heavenly smell of them! There has been absolutely nothing ever invented that came even close to smelling like a basketful of newly washed and dried clothes. These were folded and the starched items dampened for ironing. The heavier clothes were now having their turn on the lines.

Now to try and catch up on the daily things. Coal oil lamps had to be filled and the glass globes cleaned. Beds had to be made. Most of the baking having been used up over the weekend, a cake and a pan of biscuits were placed in the oven for the evening meal. Supper was cooking when the last line of clothes was brought in.

After supper, there were the outside chores, dishes and all the things that had been neglected during the day. At nine o'clock the other half would decide he had had a hard day and was off to bed. "By the way, Vern," he would call over his shoulder, "What did you do with yourself all day?"

Another type of washing was on a large-scale basis. It was the washing of the quilts and blankets. Mother picked a nice sunny day for this. The wash boiler of water was heated on the stove. Outside we kids pumped and filled large tubs of water to heat in the sun for rinsing. By the time the water was hot inside, the water in the tubs had warmed considerably. Two tubs of water were set up and a quantity of soap, enough to make suds, was stirred into the water. The quilts were then put in.

My brother Jack and I then jumped into the tub in our bare feet and tramped those quilts clean. What fun we had! We splashed and slopped and threw suds and made a fantastic job of washing. They were not so easy to wring out. Two adults were needed for this. Each one took an end and twisted until most of the water was squeezed out. The rinsing followed much the same as the washing. It was the only time we could splash and throw water to our heart's content without getting reprimanded. Jack and I loved quilt-washing day!

The soap was bar soap, sliced thin and stirred on the back of the stove with hot water until it melted. It was very often homemade soap. We loved this because it made the skin so soft and nice. To make the soap, we saved all of our excess fat. It contained just any kind that was on hand. We had the suet from the beef intestines, pork fat, bacon fat, and fat from the deer and moose we occasionally had. We put a measured amount at room temperature into a warmed ten-gallon crock. It had to be enamel, china or crockery because when the lye was added it was liquid fire. We used another crock for the lye and water. The water was cold when the lye was added, making a SWOOSH and HISS when mixed. It was done outside if possible. If you ever were unlucky enough to have some splash on your flesh, it would cause a nasty deep burn. The Gillette lye mixture was added to the fat in the large crock and stirred with a large wooden spoon or paddle, again being very careful with the first part. As soon as the mix came together and was stirred, it thickened right up to the consistency of play dough. Containers had been prepared beforehand and lined with white cloth. The quickly thickening soap was poured into these containers. In a couple of hours we could cut it into suitable sizes, usually with a wire.

If you had very delicate fat and perfumes, you could include some perfume, or even colour and make toilet soap, or go a little farther and have fancy moulds.

I was in my twenties when I saw my first soap flakes. Bar soap was used for doing the dishes, scrubbing the floor, doing the laundry and all of the odd jobs that came along. Never having enough homemade soap, we used P. & G. or Comfort bar soap. During the war, I was the envy of my neighbours, being the only one in our area who never ran out of soap. Whenever I had enough fat, I would make a batch to tide me over until I had enough coupons to buy more.

MY FATHER – HIS TALENTS

One of the most talented persons I have known in my lifetime was my father. But it was not until my adult years that I fully appreciated the many things to which he could turn his hand. In my younger years we just took this for granted; it was just things that any normal person could do, or so we thought.

Born in 1867 in Peterhead, Scotland, he was the oldest child. Six years later they emigrated to the U.S. A few years later they moved on to Ontario. He died at 93.

My father went to school part time for only five or six years; education in those days was of only secondary importance. It was worked in around the weather, work, and keeping food on the table. It was not easy to walk two miles to school with insufficient clothing and sometimes not enough food, in minus 20 to 40 degree weather.

My earliest memories of my father are of him doing something, in the evenings, with wood – carving or making articles. We were farmers but he loved the woodworking most of all. He made everything from small toys to barns and houses. I can remember one evening, we were all sitting around doing whatever job had been assigned to us. My mother and I were knitting. "Jim", she said, "I need larger needles than any that I have". After asking what size she required, he set about making a pair. They were perfect in gauge when he had finished and it seemed like a very short time.

My brother and I used to marvel, in later years, how a man with so little education could lay out a barn frame in sections on the ground and on barn raising day have it all go together and fit perfectly. There was no second chance.

Dad had in his workshop neck yokes, whiffle trees, single or double trees, axe handles, hammer handles, and many, many other items. When a less talented neighbour came to visit he was usually given any one of the items which he needed. In those days there were no money transactions. The favour would be returned in some other way. My father made us sleighs, bob sleds, skis, a checker board, cribbage board, and crocinole board. The pegs were made of cut off 2" nails, but who cared! Those crocinoles surely bounced. He made a library set for Mother. The two chairs were of pure oak and took truck driver muscles to move. The sets were covered with leather and stuffed with horse hair. The base of the table was oak with the top in maple to make it a trifle lighter.

In later days when there were grandchildren, they received rocking horses, table and chair sets, wheel barrows, and much more. When we were small, there was not time enough for these things, and in our small house, not enough room.

He kept his tools razor sharp; in fact many hours were spent by all of us in turning the grindstone while he sharpened axes, hoes, spoke shaves, drawknives, etc. He sure knew how to bear down to test our muscles. When we were small we were all forbidden to touch his sharp tools, but kids will be kids. One day at the age of seven, Jack decided he could make a pretty good slice of a piece of timber lying temptingly there. He picked up the drawknife and with his hands firmly gripped on the handles, he brought it towards him and right into his knee, leaving a scar he carried for the rest of his life. But believe me, his knee was not the sorest part of his body that evening. Dad was always on a very short fuse and had very little patience with us.

Ropes were used in all aspects of farming and most of the time there was no money to replace them. Everyone learned the art of splicing at an early age. The most expensive of all was the rope that was used to unload the bundles of hay from the wagon to the haymow. Then there was the long one that went from the hayfork at the wagon to the rafters and on into the haymow. He could make a splice that would last for years. Not very handsome, but totally useful.

He made sleds, not the greatest for sleigh riding fun but much better than most of the kids had. These were a great utility sled. They were used to haul groceries, move 100 pound bags of feed and many other things on the farm. He made us lighter bob sleighs for fun. What a grand time we had! We used to see how many bodies we could pile on. There were many upsets, but that was just part of the fun. An evening wasn't complete without a few tumbles.

We used the utility sled for a dog sled. Two of my brothers were great dog trainers. They always trained our current dog or dogs to pull the sleigh. At one time, my brother Jack brought back from the lumber camp, a year old female that was half wolf. It had belonged to an old trapper there and he was anxious to be rid of it. Jack would never, until he died, be without a dog. So he brought Queenie home. I never gave it a second thought that it might be dangerous to drive a part wolf dog. I love dogs and have never in my life been afraid of one. If they are vicious, I respect that, and never go near. But I have had many so called cross dogs come on their own to me to be patted. One day I went out to harness Queenie to take her to town to bring home the groceries. I had on a coat that I didn't usually wear. Before I could get her completely harnessed, she went right for my throat. I fended her off with no damage except a couple of fang marks in one leg. I went back to the house and found my mother in near hysterics. This was a most unusual state for my unflappable mother. We came to the conclusion when I was removing my coat, that it had a WOLF collar and that was Queenie's trouble. I put on another coat and continued to harness Queenie. Mother was still agitated and tried to persuade me to stay home. I was about nineteen at the time. Queenie was very friendly to me and for the years that I stayed at home she never was anything but a great family dog.

Dad of course had made all of the harness for the dogs, mostly from discarded horse harness.

Dad was also great at blacksmith work, leather work, and making rope. He soled and repaired our shoes, patched and mended harness. When he did leather work, he made his own thread from beeswax and hemp. Leather was often taken from some worn out article. An old leather shoe that had gone beyond any visible use had the tops made into shoe laces. Leather was sometimes bought by the side (beef) but cost us much more money than we usually could come up with. It was mostly a square or piece of leather that we could afford at the time. He made much of the harness that we used, and was always replacing some worn-out part. He could always find a way to make something to make a job a little easier. I think now if he had put his mind to it, he could have given Thomas Edison a run for his money.

Later I married another farmer, but he had little dexterity for woodwork. It was then I began to appreciate the talents that I was used to. When we were married, my dad made us a set of heavy working sleighs; every bit hand made. He had the local blacksmith do the iron work on them. My husband really prized them and it was with deep regret that we sold them when we decided to move to Southern Ontario. My husband summed it up when he was making a very rough version of a sorely needed ironing board. “You know, Vern” he said, “I might have done a better job of it if I hadn’t kept looking over my shoulder all the time, afraid that your dad might suddenly appear”.

Jim Thom in Alberta, with a friend.

Although Dad never owned a car, here he seems to enjoy trying one out! This picture has a story.

On 1911 or 1912, Dad went to Alberta to work at harvesting. It was quite common to do that then. They had special trains (at special rates) that took hundreds of people for the four to six weeks needed to harvest the crop. Dad had thoughts of moving there but Mom didn’t like the idea. While he was there he sat in a motor car for the first time. Then he wanted to have his picture taken, and sent it to Mom.

Next year was when the house burned.

SUMMER OF THE HAWK

Poultry were always a very necessary part of our lives. Cash was almost non existent. Eggs and butter were bartered for credit. With lack of refrigeration, the basements were the only cool place to keep the butter and eggs at the store and they had to do a quick turn over to ensure their freshness.

Every farm lady had her little flock of poultry. This, and her butter, was the very backbone of the home. It was most essential that there were eggs and butter to barter.

We would have twenty or thirty laying hens; that is if we were lucky. They were left to roam all over and picked up a certain amount of their feed, insects and seeds, in the fields and yard. We were often sent to find where a few hens were hiding their nests. We would rob the nests and bring back the treasured eggs. New chicks were hatched by setting hens. First of all you had to wait for a hen to get broody and give her an extra couple of days to make sure she didn't change her mind. Then she was put into a dark place, covered with a bushel basket leaving it propped up enough for her to leave if she wished. Sometimes you might not have a broody hen and your neighbour had more than she needed. A broody hen was not laying, therefore unless she was raising a family, she was a detriment. A laying hen could be traded for her, then a dozen eggs were carefully selected and placed beneath her.

The hatching period was three weeks. You were lucky if, at the end of the season, you had raised six or eight chicks from each broody hen. It took a long time to build up a flock of new layers. It was unheard of to buy chicks; and no one had money for buying poultry anyway. If you had four broody hens, you might, if you were lucky, raise twenty-five new chicks. Half of these would be roosters. Then there were always a few older hens that had to hit the stew pot, as they were not productive layers. The broody hens were out of production for the season, as they still had to raise those chicks, and would probably not lay again until next spring. Sometimes one of the hens would have only a couple of chicks and the mother hen could get careless and step on these. If there were two small batches we would try to put them together with the most responsible mother. Some, like human mothers, would take them; others were really vicious and were quite indignant when asked to raise the orphans. The excused mother could be back in production soon if relieved of her charges.

Our hen houses were raided occasionally by foxes or weasels, but it was usually a one time thing. We always had a good watchdog, so that the raider was discouraged from coming back for a second try.

One year, which later became known as the Summer of the Hawk, we had a very smart hawk that did some surveillance on our place and liked what he saw. We had no money to buy poultry fencing, so there was no way we could keep the chickens safe, short of keeping them shut in the hen house, where they would have perished from the heat. In a couple of weeks, that hawk had sadly depleted our little flock. He was so adept that he was in and gone before you realized it. He must have been a nice fat bird by the end of the summer. Mom set some of us younger kids to watching for him while we went about our jobs of piling wood or working the garden. We really tried but that hawk was smarter than we were.

We were down to two chicks, when Dad decided to get involved. He had a most explosive temper at all times and he was not in the mood to let some bird out smart him. He decided to devote his time for the next few days to splitting wood, as it was near the poultry. He kept a shot gun beside him and was all set. He was a crack shot and it should be a cinch to blow that meddling bird right out of orbit; or so he thought!

Everything went well the first day. Dad thought he had the answer. After all, it was just a matter of being in the right spot until he showed that bird who was boss on this farm! He picked up his gun and went into the house. As he stepped through the doorway, that hawk swooped down and grabbed the next to last chick. By the time Dad got out, it had glided behind the barn and was away. Dad had miscalculated the bird's bedtime.

Next day, he kept the gun beside him until almost noon. By now Dad had kept working and decided to move to the other side of the woodpile. He was now at least ten feet from his gun. Well quicker than a wink, that hawk was there, snatched our last chicken and was out of sight! Dad was in such a rage that he was kicking and ranting at everything in sight! The words that emerged from him were never ever meant for our tender ears, even though we were used to his language! "That G---D------------- hawk, he DID get the best of me!" he screamed.

BURIED TREASURES

Remember going to the fairs and picnics and dipping your hands into a barrel of sawdust? You paid a nickel and were allowed to delve into that sawdust. Your heart was beating and you were so excited! Perhaps it would be something extra special this time. The prizes were wrapped and well padded with newspapers so that we could not distinguish them by the feel. They never were exactly what you had anticipated (probably because we had set our sights too high). There were cheap jewellery, doll clothes, marbles, games, or perhaps a tin horn. A whistle was always popular for the boys. Times haven't changed very much, for even sixty or more years ago the boys liked to whistle at the girls.

One day recently while grocery shopping, I was passing the oatmeal section. The image of yesterday flashed across my mind. I wanted to pick up a package and feel it. Yes – feel it! For inside there was a piece of china, or so my mind told me.

Back in the early twenties and thirties, newly weds had very few dishes to begin their new home. In every package of oatmeal there was a dish, usually of a charming pattern. This was a very slow process of building up a dinner set, especially when you were a family of two. In our family, there were always seven or eight, plus the many visitors we always had. A box of oatmeal didn't last long and we soon could look forward to another box of oatmeal and another dish. Mother would come home and start disposing the groceries. We kids could hardly wait. Was it a dinner plate? That was where the feeling part came in; if you pushed the side edges together, you could feel the edge of a dinner plate. Bread and butter plates were hard to guess, as was a saucer, cereal bowl or fruit nappy. A cup could also be felt by squeezing the flat sides. Dinner plates and cups were the most popular, but a real prize was a vegetable bowl. The grocer was usually very good-natured about letting you pick your own. Being a real Scots family, we never ever started the day without porridge.

When soap flakes became popular, they started packing dishes into soap packages. They then decided to make a change, and included a towel or dish towel. These were always useful but there was no suspense. We did miss the feeling and anticipation. Many of the grocery packages over the years, contained glassware that is now referred to as DEPRESSION GLASS. Some of it was very beautiful, but some was very ugly, depending, I suppose, on the eye of the beholder or how badly you needed it. Most of the women tried to build up a complete set.

One of the most striking to my eyes was a little cream jug from the oatmeal. It was white with a few cornflowers decorating one side, and on the other, one flower. It was the shape of the little jug that was so eye-catching. It was tall, thin, but just a wee bit pot-bellied and held about six or eight ounces. Several years ago, I was at a yard sale and found one. It was in excellent shape and I bought it. I couldn't resist. I kept it in a place where I could always see it. After a couple of years, I decided to give it to my granddaughter who loves antiques and Gram's stories.

GRANDPARENTS

Grandparents were a scarce commodity in my childhood. Two of them died years before I was born and my maternal grandfather lived about 200 miles away. Travel was expensive in those days and the time to travel was hard to find.

Grandfather Fisher was a farmer just as we were. He had seven girls and two boys, my mother being the second child. My only memory of him was when I was 14 years of age. He came and spent Christmas with us. He was a lovely, caring gentleman, and we quite liked him. I remember the evening before he left us to go home, the family was gathered around the fire. He went around to each of us and gave us all a great big hug; and in those days, hugs were not quite so plentiful as they are now. He lived for another five years, but that is the only memory I have of him. It is a very pleasant memory and I have often wished I had seen him more often.

The other grandparent I remember slightly, was my paternal grandmother. She was someone special. She did all the nursing and doctoring for a radius of 20 miles. She delivered babies, sewed up wounds, treated pneumonia, set broken bones, and just anything else that came up. Her family at home always managed to cope while Grandma Thom was away. There were older ones who could cope. Neither the rains in summer nor the storms in winter kept her home when she was needed. Transportation was the horse and buggy or a cutter, whatever the season. When these were impossible, it was snowshoes or on foot.

For over 30 years, a baby was not born, in that area, which was not delivered by this marvellous lady. No money was ever received for her work. Many things were given to her, such as vegetables, eggs, or a roast, when people felt they would like to repay her. It was sometimes just a token but it was graciously received.

I know I must have seen Grandmother quite often for she lived just a mile away, but I have only one memory of her. My seven-year-old brother and I were sent to deliver some items to her home. She had suffered a stroke shortly before and had difficulty in speaking. The majority of her children were married by this time, except one girl who was a little below normal, and the youngest son, so she had a hired girl. Grandma sat in her favourite rocking chair near the kitchen stove rocking and trying to talk to us. We had heard so many stories of her helpfulness that it was sad, even at our age, to see her so helpless.

We shyly went in to greet Grandmother. She was able to give us a one armed hug, but we could not understand even one word she said. How frustrating it must have been for her! Her mind was excellent, but she was unable to converse normally with us. On our visit, we had been told before we left home not to stay too long as it might tire her, so like the good little kids (ahem) we were, we said we had to go home. Grandma, at our announcement, became very agitated and kept pointing over to the kitchen cupboard. It finally dawned on the hired girl what she wanted. She was noted for her hospitality and all her life had a couple of cakes in her cupboard. She wanted Jack and me each to have a piece of cake, and when we sat happily munching, she sat smiling at us.

I was the seventh child. When I was five and a half, brother Jim, the last of the family was born. Mother was pregnant with him when Grandma Thom took the stroke. Mom loved her mother-in-law very dearly and didn't want to worry her, so she never told her she was pregnant. Grandma died in December, just a couple of months after Jack's and my visit to her. Mom and Dad were there with her at the last. Mom could always understand her slurred speech. Near the last she beckoned my mother to her and said: "I am so sorry Bella that I can't live long enough to deliver this last child for you." Mom often told us this and her eyes had a tear in them because she too would have liked to see her last child delivered by Grandmother Thom.

HOME COMFORTS

Have you ever wondered just how our forebears managed their sickness and accidents without the presence of a doctor? In the early days doctors were few and far between in the more isolated places. Where we lived, it was fifteen miles to the closest doctor, and the next nearest was 50 miles. So if your nearest was away on a call in the other direction, or ill, you just had to do your best with what you had.

My dad's family moved to the Spanish area about 1890. Wherever she lived, my Grandmother did the doctoring and nursing. Just a few years ago when reading their family history, I realized where she received her interest in healing. Her uncle and two brothers were doctors. One settled in Hartford, Connecticut, and the other in Vancouver; in fact there is a memorial to him in North Vancouver. This was not for his doctoring, but for another reason altogether.

Grandma Thom went wherever she was called. She nursed flu, contagious diseases, accidents, broken bones, and sutures – wherever she was needed. She delivered almost every baby in the area. I can't give you any of her cures and remedies as I was only five when she died but she never refused a call.

One of the greatest standbys was goose grease. It was rubbed on our chests for almost anything. We must have smelled to high heaven. If we did we scarcely noticed, probably because everyone else smelled the same. My mother was a most fastidious person, but she put up with the smells even if she agreed the cure was almost worse than the disease. She was never put off by the severity of an accident or an ailment. She was a great person in an emergency.

We had castor oil, another popular item, as was steeped senna leaves, and Epsom salts for bowel ailments. We used to gag on these. But if we point blank refused, it did us no good as our noses were held and then we had to drink it. If we complained about the taste, we were reminded that if it didn't taste bad it wouldn't cure you. A chest cold in the winter was to be avoided if possible because we knew the consequences of that. Our chests were rubbed with Capsolin, a remedy that was red hot on our chests, guaranteed to kill or cure. This was unimaginable torture to tender young chests and would leave us with blistered skin. As soon as Mother left the room, we jumped out of bed, took our pillow and put against the frosted window pane and then on to our burning skin. It helped, if only temporarily. We would have lost a little skin from another part if we had been caught. Just remember, no pain – no gain. She also used mustard plasters.

Everyone had his own cure for hiccoughs. Drink two glasses of cold water as fast as you could; drink a glass of water upside down; or sometimes a bad scare would be an instant cure. We all tried to think up new scare tactics to use. These were only a few. There were also as many cures for snoring. If anyone asked me today a good cure for snoring, I would give them the 100% fool proof cure – separate bedrooms!

Iodine, Mercurochrome and peroxide were used for all cuts and open wounds. Lysol, or carbolic acid, was used liberally for disinfecting.

Boils were very common and were always poulticed. Linseed, bread and milk, and many more poultices were used. There were a few who used cob webs, cow dung and more unmentionables. We didn't know these troublesome boils were caused by a poor diet.

In the spring, our blood had to be cleansed so the best cure for that was molasses and sulphur. Of course you had no close friends as long as you were imbibing this cure.

Laudanum was used for severe pain and was doled out very carefully, and then locked away. For a toothache, there was oil of cloves. Some of the men swore by chewing tobacco for a toothache. Many of the men I knew must never have had a toothache in their lives for they were addicted tobacco chewers. Heat was always used, either a jar of hot water or a heated brick. For a sore throat, Mother used to paint our throats with something on a feather. I know it was something commonly used, but for the life of me I can't remember what it was.

There were cures for warts, ringworm, and impetigo. I know lard and sulphur was used on some of these. Each housewife had her own homemade ointment. The basis of most of these was goose grease.

Friends shared what they had with the neighbours. Perhaps someone had run out of goose grease, or Epsom salts, heaven forbid, but no self respecting house wife would ever run out of castor oil or sulphur.

I can remember one incident when I was about five, when we were out sleigh riding. We went to a forbidden place because the hill was great for us. At the foot of the hill was a barbed wire fence. The older boys had looped it up. They would keep their heads down until they had passed under it, then bob up. They would not let me ride my sleigh, as I was too small. One day, seven-year-old Jack bobbed up too soon. He tore his both lips severely. Dr. Flaherty, the nearest doctor, came to sew it up. He came in a horse and cutter. Later he returned to remove the stitches. As he told Jack that he was a real hero in not making a fuss, he dropped change into Jack's hand; this was almost half of his fee. Dr. Flaherty was very gruff and loved by everyone around. He had the most marvellous sense of humour. Fifty years later people could still be heard repeating Doc Flaherty jokes and stories. He had an inexhaustible supply.

In the bad flu epidemic of 1919, I was three years old. My mother complained to Dr. Flaherty that I only asked for fat pork (I can't imagine it). He instantly replied, "Good God, woman, give it to her. If she can't digest it she will puke it up."

When I was about six or seven, I decided the stove needed more fuel. Everyone was busy in another area. I, being an independent soul, (and still am) decided to do it myself instead of asking for help. My arms were used to work but were not up to balancing the lid as I moved it. I was not too much taller than the stove at that time. I took the stove lifter and struggled to remove the lid. The lid had a mind of its own and rolled over and on one of my bare feet. I can remember, when I was lying in bed after receiving first aid, my mother knowing my love of lilacs brought a large bouquet of them into my room. This was unheard of to have flowers in your bedroom. I was in terrific pain but really appreciated the lilacs. I still think of this every time I smell lilacs. It is a nice memory.

People had ways of dealing with emergencies that would be unheard of now. When my grandmother started leaving her family to care for the smaller ones, this worked out quite well except when she had a deliver a new baby and had to stay away overnight. One time, when her second last baby was only a few months old, she was called about ten miles away to nurse a case of pneumonia. She went by horse and cutter and had to walk the last mile. Her neighbour, Mrs. Muncaster had a baby the same age. She took Grandma Thom's baby and nursed them both while she was away. Mrs. Muncaster's baby, when he grew up, became my uncle as he married Grandma Thom's last child. Grandma Thom's baby grew to six foot three, and Willy Muncaster never grew more than five foot seven. It was a standing joke with Willy that my Uncle John had stolen most of his mother's milk when they were babies and that accounted for his short stature.

THRESHING TIME

When the days became shorter in the summer, we kids were thinking, or in the case of the boys, trying to avoid thinking, of school; the adults were thinking of threshing time.

Threshing time was a very busy time for both men and women. The threshing was done with a steam engine. This was a very heavy, awkward vehicle and took two teams of horses to pull it. It used up a terrific amount of water. The kids were sent to fill up the 50 gallon barrels of water. These were set up close to the engine. Sometimes we kids carried it. If we were small, it took us all afternoon and many aching muscles to fill it. If the older boys were home and not on another job, they would use a horse and barrels. The barrels would be put on a sloop, or stone boat, and drawn over to the job. That didn't happen very often, as Dad didn't give us much sympathy for sore aching bodies. The men had to bring in a huge supply of wood to make the steam. The wood was delivered to the site with a horse.

The thresher of my childhood was Bob Gamble. There was only the one thresher in our area, who served not only our community but also several others. He would start in August and probably not be home until November. Bob had several sons at home to carry on the workload. Sometimes one would accompany him for awhile if he could be spared. The money was always a welcome source of income. Bob's wife Nell, was the mid-wife after my Grandmother passed away.

Usually a neighbour, or sometimes two, would come and give a hand with the serving and washing up the day of the threshing. The women would get caught up on the latest gossip. It was a way of life that both men and women did most of their catching up on current events while working.

Mom would make a trip to the store for supplies for her baking. This cut into the time needed to get ready for the next day. Perhaps a ham was bought. Sometimes Dad butchered a lamb. No one I ever knew could do justice to a roast of lamb like my mother. She would make a roux of butter and flour and coat the roast. I know my family doesn't like lamb, but then they never tasted real lamb. When, in later years, on our way to New Zealand, we were asked who liked lamb, there were three out of thirty who did. The twenty-seven others said they had no intention of eating any. Our second night in Rotarua, we were taken to a private home for dinner, three or four to a home. They had a committee to do this and were paid by our travel agents. They had a special standard to follow. Four of us were taken to the President's home. We had a fabulous meal. When we came home, and were discussing it, the other three thought they were eating pork and hadn't a clue they were eating lamb. Before a week had gone by, the thirty people in our group were ordering lamb when they had plenty of other choices. They probably didn't like what the stores offered here when they arrived home. There is just no comparison. The lamb we were served in New Zealand tasted just like Mom's.

Kneeling: Ron Thaxter, Max Witty, George Robinson, Ron Erickson, Ken Fairbairn. Top Row: Lorne Caldwell, Jim Tracy, Frank Witty, Jim with Warren, Dune Fairbairn, Alex Driver, Joe Roach, Alec Hannah. Threshing machine in background.

There was much to do the day before the threshers arrived. Potatoes, carrots, turnips, and cabbage for coleslaw were gathered from the garden. There was the inevitable trip to the store. It wasn't that we couldn't have gone earlier, knowing we would need supplies, but that we had no refrigeration. There were usually about ten or twelve pies to bake. Then there was a cake or two and cookies. And of course there was always bread to be made. The smells and odours of these goodies would nearly drive us kids crazy. We thought we couldn't possibly wait until the next day. We would beg Mom to let us help but she would always say, "Just keep out of my way." We never could understand how that would help her. We were sure if we could get near the food preparations, a little taste testing wouldn't go amiss. Years later, when I had a family of my own, I finally understood her logic.

The neighbour who came to help would usually bring something of her own. It might be baking or her favourite pickles or fruit. The vegetables were always cleaned and prepared the night before, and the baking of course. We women had milking and chores to do, so there was rather a long day before and a long one the day of the threshing. Those hard working men had some appetite! They could do away with an amount in one day that would feed your modern male office worker for a week.

It wasn't always this good for the men. There was the odd housewife who was just not a good cook and at least two ladies who had not the mental capacity to be able to cook well for any number of people. The men could hardly wait to finish there and get on with the next one where the food was better. They worked very hard and long. The large amount they consumed was needed to keep them going.

There were ethnic differences in the food served. We had quite a few German people. They served sauerkraut, strudels, sausage etc. A family living near us said they used several barrels of sauerkraut over the winter. There would be about thirty or forty gallons per barrel. Mrs. Hocher, when she came to visit us, always brought some with her. They served it at every meal all year round. Even though we made some ourselves, hers always tasted different. Another family was French and they always had pea soup. They used three or more hundred pound bags of peas each season.

The men also did their catching up visits at this time. By the time they had threshed at nine or ten places, they would have gone through a whole year's worth of gossip. But threshing was a dirty, hard job. If the straw was blown outside into a stack, it was a relatively simple job to keep the blower making a fair sized straw stack; but if there was room in the haymow for the straw, it was almost impossible to work there. The heat was almost unbearable, and the dust excruciating. No one wanted that job. It was unbelievable the amount of dust and dirt that went into the lungs and throat. They all hated the dreaded barley. It was worse than handling thistles.

When the men trooped in for a meal, they washed up outside. We kept a fresh supply of towels for them, but just using them once, made them filthy. By the time they had washed up for their second meal of the day, we were just about out of fresh ones.

The year I turned twenty, my mother was sick in bed for a week. A girl my own age came to help me the day of the threshing. Baking and cooking for a gang was no new thing to me. I had taken over the cooking and the heavy load of family responsibilities at fourteen. Mother's health was not too great at that time.

When the men came in someone yelled: "Young cooks today." Everything went well until I drained the potatoes. As I was transferring them to bowls, the pot (about a ten-quart size) flipped over and all the potatoes went on the floor. I had a large roast of beef and lovely brown gravy. The men would have been happy to make a meal of this, along with the potatoes, if need be, but this day they were deprived of their potatoes. All I could do was just work around it hoping I wouldn't slide in them until I had the meal on the table. One man, not to be daunted by a pile of boiled potatoes on the floor took his plate and fork over and helped himself to some off the top. The balance of the men did not have his panache so did with large slices of bread from the day before.

When the men had gone, the evening chores were tackled. There was always the milking, stock to feed and the separator to wash up. It would be great if I could say we rested just a tad the next day, but no such luck. The men had to go on to the next neighbour to be threshed and the lady of the house usually went there also to give a hand. Then, of course, there was the custom of bringing some baking. It was not easy to come up with something after having had so many men to feed the day before. The leftovers (if any) were used to feed her own family at home. Usually she could come up with something in the line of pickles that was not too common and would be a treat for the others. Each housewife seemed to have a speciality that most of the others didn't.

In later years, when my husband was living and both of us working, I would, in the morning, put our dinner in the oven, set the timer and come home to appetizing smells as I pulled into the driveway. It was like having a maid.

I often wonder how we would make out now, cooking for threshers, with our electricity, freezers, supermarkets with choices and ready cooked items, and money to spend on them. At that time, we would have been unable to secure those items as we could not afford them if they had been offered. Instead, the baking was all done with a wood stove. I can still remember the overwhelming heat put forth by the old cook stove. I am now amazed at the size of the ovens they possessed, they were so small! I was looking at one just recently and of course the first thought was how had we ever cooked for so many people in such a sized oven. However, it was never empty for the whole day. The only hot water we had was (if we were lucky) a reservoir on the right hand side of the stove. It never got very hot except when the oven was in constant use. All other water was heated in large pots on the top of the stove.

Cookies were baked a few days ahead, perhaps a fruitcake also. But the pies and cakes were done the day before. No meal for the threshers would be complete without the pies. Everything else took second place. There were apple, raisin, pumpkin, blueberry, raspberry, custard, cream and a few rare specialities. There was usually a pot of beans cooking slowly in the oven, usually left there in the evening after the other baking was done. They would be left there all night. Everyone loved baked beans.

Amazingly there were not too many oversized people. They just burned those thousands of calories into oblivion and didn't worry about it.

BOB AND ROY

My favourite of all the farm animals I grew up with was a pair of strawberry roans, named Bob and Roy. I had been going over some old pictures at my brother's house when I ran across a snapshot of them. The memories came pouring back and with a lot of "Do you remember the time" with my two brothers and myself, incidents kept on pouring in. The horses were half brothers and were bought a couple of years before I was born at about two and three years of age. We had them until I was about twenty. They were almost part of our family. Never in over forty years of farming have any animals made such an impact on our lives.

They were not large as horses go. They were very gentle and had each his very own personality. Roy was a real gentleman, kind and caring, while Bob was quick to take offence and always jealous. If Bob was petted first, all was well, you could then make a big fuss over Roy and he stood there and gently waited his turn again. But if first you went to Roy, then watch out, for Bob would remind you with a gentle nip that he came first. One time my sister picked some nice fresh grass and made the mistake of presenting it to Roy. Bob reached over and nipped her shoulder. He did it a little harder than usual and left marks. It was unusual for him to do anything but give a little reminder. However, he must have regretted his action that day, for he never tried it again. Then there was the day that my brother Cliff took a shortcut over the manger into the feed alley. Just as he was climbing over, Bob gave him a little nip on the seat of the pants to help him along. Cliff swore that Bob laughed at him.

We learned to ride horse back on them. We always enjoyed a little ride on our way home from a day in the fields. They were so gentle that our parents never worried about us riding them at a very tender age. Our biggest problem was finding a handy stump or piece of machinery, (or even an older sibling) to climb aboard.

Verna on Roy, left, and Jack on Bob, right. This picture was taken when the horses were first purchased.

We were always around the horses. One day my dad thought Roy had something wrong with a foot, until he noticed that I, a seven year old was too close and Roy would not put that foot down until I moved out of the way.

Another time, my five-year-old brother disappeared from the house, and after hunting in all the likely places, my mother went to the stables. Bob was

Jim, on the left, taken at the lumber camp.

Warren ready for a ride on the load of logs. Blackie is already on the load – he went wherever Jim went. The horses are "Beauty" and "Silver", Jim's special ladies.

standing there demanding his supper, but Roy was lying down with Jim asleep on his back. Roy, being the gentleman that he was, would not get up until my mother removed Jim.

My father worked in the lumber camps every winter with the horses. They were badly spoiled by the men. Everyone liked them and made much of feeding them. They played up Bob's jealousy just to get a laugh. They were fed cookies, bread and their favourite, tobacco. They weren't fussy whether it was smoking or chewing. It was a habit they hated to give up when they came home. One day Cliff had the team at the village after delivering a load of wood. As he stood talking to a friend, they moved around in front of the horses. Bob reached out and helped himself to the package of roll your owns in Ted's pocket.

When he was well in his twenties, Dad sold Roy to an old bachelor about five miles away. This was a very hard thing to do.

We were very poor as it was still depression days and we could not afford to keep another horse that was unable to put in a hard day's work. The gentleman who bought

Jim in the lumber camp (J. J. McFadden Lumber, north of Blind River). Jim loved working with horses.

him was very good to him. He was retired. He had a bush lot and cut his own wood. He used Roy to haul out his wood for his own use and to plough the garden. It was a job that Roy was still able to do. His working hours probably averaged about one or two hours a week of very light jobs. A real horse heaven!

One morning about a year later, when the men went to the stable to do their morning chores, there stood Roy in his old stall. He had decided to come home to his family.

STORES ON WHEELS

In the early twenties, we looked forward to seeing the tinkers. Farm people are very busy people, and in the busy summer season had very little time for visiting. So it was quite an event when a new visitor appeared at our home, especially if it happened to be one from some distance away.

The tinker's vehicle was a light covered wagon drawn by a pair of horses. Their wagons held a great assortment of small items. There were ribbons, pins, lace, thread and yard goods. Also included were other items: some pots, pans, dishes and many goods that a busy housewife might like, as well as the necessities. He also sharpened knives and scissors. What excitement for us kids! This was better for us than a trip to the store. In the store you could see everything at a glance, but here you never knew what was in those boxes and parcels until the tinker brought them out and let us see their wonders.

Money was tight, but we always managed to buy something; some thread, buttons, yard goods, ric rac braid, or brightly coloured wool. The tinker usually stayed for a cup of tea and a piece of cake. He knew the latest news of our more far away neighbours, and kept on gathering newsworthy items as he went along. Because he covered a large area, there was time for only one visit per year. I don't know what he did in the off season, but when spring appeared, so did our tinker. I know we always looked forward to his visits. We always hoped he hadn't forgotten us or would not be calling on us this year. I cannot remember when he last visited.

Then in the late twenties and early thirties, this time by a light van type car, there appeared the Daly Tea man. He usually visited us twice a year, early spring and late fall. He was happily welcomed as we used a great amount of tea. He sold his products in bulky packages and it was much more reasonable to buy in large lots. If, luckily, we had some cash on hand, we bought quite a supply.

Our other regular visitors included the Rawleigh and Watkins dealers. The Watkins man had household items as well as animal cures. These were a trifle more expensive than the store ones, but we usually bought one or another of their wares. During our married years on the farm, my husband swore by the ointment and liniment for the stock. We bought mineral for the animals in 50 pound bags. We became friends with the Watkins dealer. He had the route for many years. Then after he had some ill health, his wife would come along to do the driving. After her husband's death, she took the route over herself and was still selling when we sold the farm.

When Jim and I were married we lived six miles from town. It was during the war and we did not have a car. We really appreciated the tradesmen who called.

We had two favourite people who came to us. The first was a man who was just beginning a butcher business in Sudbury. He appeared one day asking if we had some animals for sale. He confided that he didn't know anyone in the area and began asking where he might purchase beef on the hoof.

His father and two brothers were medical doctors and he was expected to follow in their footsteps. The world around him shattered when he announced his intention to become a butcher.

He had only been in business a couple of months when we first knew him, and he had almost no backing. He found he could buy a bit cheaper this way. My husband was the type of man who never met a stranger. He offered to go with Andre and take him to places where he knew there were cattle for sale. This saved time. He butchered the cattle and took them back to the butcher shop. Jim always helped him. Andre usually had dinner with us and if delayed, stayed overnight.

The first time he stayed over, he asked if we would waken him early. He should never have said that to my husband! Jim was up most days shortly after five. Early, to him was four o'clock, and that was the time he awakened Andre. Later we had many laughs over this. Andre was very good to us and repaid us in many ways. We became great friends.

Another one who comes to mind is a man from Sudbury who came once a month with a van and a beautiful supply of dry goods. We became good friends until we moved away. He would often stay for a meal. We never would let him pay for it, but almost always, there were a few goodies left for us for our hospitality. I purchased work clothing, for our two children and ourselves, plus many household items.

His prices were very reasonable. He was never in a hurry and never pushed his wares. The goods that he sold were always of number one quality. When you had made your selection, he would look it over and say: "I see you have quite a few items here, so we had better do something about that." He either gave us a reduced price or gave us free items. Perhaps he had seen us admiring them earlier. He sold a great deal in his travels. On one visit he had extra supplies of wool. Knitting and crocheting have always been my most favourite pastime. This was autumn so I was buying wool for sweaters, mittens and small things. He mentioned that he was always left with a box or two of "orphans", the end of colours or dye lots. Wool was selling for about 25 cents a ball at the time and he gave me the reduced price of 10 cents. This was indeed a great bargain. At the end of his visit, he said if I would buy the lot that he had left, he would reduce it still further. Knowing that I had quite an amount of knitting to do, I agreed. He had more than I expected. He brought in a huge box and only charged me about two cents a ball, saying that he would have it left on his hands if I didn't take it. Not too many people loved knitting as I did in those days. It was well that I did like this job when there was so much of it to be done. My husband and I didn't keep sheep on our farm.

One visit I remember quite well, as it has become a family joke. I had bought several items of clothing for my husband, son, and daughter. Marilyn was only an infant, so her new clothing didn't excite her, but it was a different story for Warren, who was four at the time. I bought a pair of rubber boots, the smallest I had ever seen, knowing he would love them because they were just like Dad's. I also bought him jeans and shirts. When he saw his dad coming in at night, he ran to meet him, showing off his first pair of boots, and telling what else I had bought. Later, when our son was in bed, Jim asked: "What the devil are cowboy jumps?" I was just as bewildered at what cowboy jumps were until I suddenly remembered that the jeans I had bought for Warren were HOP-A-LONG Cassidys.

This salesman, with his van, probably did more business in a week, than any general store in town. I can't imagine anyone else who had the patience, understanding and tolerance of our van salesman. I have racked my brains for months trying to remember his name, and I was unsuccessful; but what is the disgrace in forgetting a name when you remember all his kindness and friendship?

Verna, Jim and son Warren.

THE MAIL ORDER CATALOGUE

Our nearest village being very small meant that we were very dependent upon the mail order catalogue. There were two stores in this village, both being in the living room of the storekeeper's home. They were very small and could carry mostly staples. One contained the post office. That store was really the gathering place for the community. You could see from the front of the postal window if there were any letters in your box. It has been known for the odd long armed person to reach inside and help himself to his own mail; that is until caught.

There was very little junk mail then. The largest bulk of mail was parcels from the Eaton's, and Simpson's catalogues. These catalogues were delivered in our mail twice a year. We eagerly looked forward to receiving them. Even though we had little money to spend, they were our Woolworth, Department, Drug and Hardware store combined. There was just about nothing you couldn't buy from them. God Bless Timothy Eaton for thinking of it! Simpson's soon followed.

In the sixties, I worked for a publisher, who had the first issue of the Eaton Catalogue. His Grandfather had been a very well known publisher and had left his collections to Chuck. He also had many of the very old Comics. When business was slack during summer months, it was my job to catalogue them. That was a job made in Heaven.

We kids fought over who would be first to pore over the new catalogue. When my brothers got their turn, they would slyly turn over to ladies undies for a peek at the pornography of the times. They hurriedly turned past it if Mom was in the vicinity.

The fall issue came out just before school time. You could send your order on Monday and receive it on Wednesday. If your order was over two dollars, they paid the postage. There were many, many things to be had for under two dollars, but the two dollars were hard to come by. The whole family took part in the making up of the order. Most people sent cash, but a money order could be purchased in the local post office. Looking back it seems like a myth that we could send cash money that way. I can never remember not receiving an order when cash was sent.

When the men came home from the lumber camps in the spring, the most urgent thing was to send off an order to purchase the necessary things. These probably should have been bought earlier but there was no money then. The next urgent time was in late August. The needed school and cold weather clothing was ordered. The money for this was made possible by the sale of wood and the first crop of potatoes.

The old catalogue was sent out to the outhouse for recycling. Many minutes were used up there catching up on things that had been missed earlier. We always held back one for us kids to play with in the house. We had games we played. Each catalogue had several pages of regular paper, then a page of colour. These coloured pages were prized by the girls. We would each take so many pages and see how many rings and jewellery we could find on these coloured ones. We cut our paper dolls from them. What fun we had!

These old catalogues were super heating pads. They were heated up in a warm oven, then tucked under an aching ear or tooth, or put under a pair of cold feet. The warmth lasted for quite awhile.

The men would order their tools and even fencing from the catalogue. Our Christmas things all came from the catalogues, except for the homemade items. It was an impressive sight at Christmas to see the parcels piled up in the post office. They filled the little cubicle and overflowed into the store, sometimes even into the other rooms of the house.

Much of the bulkier items came, not by mail, but by freight or express. It was at Christmas that the mail order came into its own. Many of our gifts were homemade, but there were always a few catalogue gifts under the tree. We always had candy and an orange. These also were purchased from Eaton's. This was the only time we ever saw an orange as the stores didn't handle them. Not too many could afford them and the stores had no refrigeration. So an orange was quite a treat.

As the families picked up their parcels, the overflow moved out to the store from the house. By the next day there were just as many again.

At church on Sundays, a new hat or dress was immediately spotted, and we could hardly wait until we arrived home to look it up in the catalogue to see how much they had paid for it. It was not uncommon to attend a dance and be very excited because you were wearing a new dress, when lo! and behold! someone else just came in wearing YOUR DRESS! This was bad enough, but the crowning indignity was if it was in the same shade. This happened quite often, because we had only the one source from which to shop and of course we all had to buy in the same price range. You couldn't lie about the price you had paid. This was the time that anyone who could sew would give herself a mental pat on the back. If we had been to a large event, we had quite a time that evening looking up everyone's new items.

Mother saved diligently all summer every cent she could save from her butter and egg money, to have enough to purchase our going back to school clothes. I shall never forget my humiliation, at the age of nine or ten when I had to wear my brother's outgrown shoes. This was only for a matter of two weeks, but for me it was a lifetime. Actually, looking back I can't remember anyone laughing or poking fun at me. We had gone barefoot all summer. When school time came, there was just not enough money to go around. Some money was soon acquired and the order went in to the catalogue for my shoes. I felt like taking them to bed with me that night.

Sending an order in to the catalogue was a family event. Not too many orders were sent from each home. First came the really essential things; if perhaps we had a wee bit left over, there might be a little treat in some form for us and it was always something all of us could enjoy. Of course, kids being the same then as now, we tried a bit of coaxing for extras.

At Christmas the store was hard put to hold so many people. The women were shopping for their Christmas cake ingredients and groceries. Some members from most families were there to pick up their parcels from the catalogue.

When the local train arrived, huffing and puffing, people began gathering at the post office. Even though there was mail for everyone, it didn't take long to sort it. Mr. Thornton quite often just passed an envelope, without putting it in their box, to the owner if he or she happened to be near the window. "There's a letter for you, Mrs. Smith, from Johnny." This message was called to a little old lady who was unable to crowd up close. Nevertheless her whole demeanour changed, with her face absolutely shining. She had been writing faithfully every week and had not heard from her son Johnny in six months. He had been a wild one in his earlier days, but lately he seemed to be more stable. She had high hopes of him settling down. She was quite willing to wait her turn at the Post Office window, secretly savouring the good news. When the crowd thinned and she stepped up to the Post Office window she had the bearing of royalty. I do believe, at that time she would not have changed places with the Queen Mother. She took her letter and holding it closely, she left the store. This would be read in private and re-read many times.

Mrs. Smith had lost two sons in World War I, a daughter in childbirth, and her husband had been deceased many years ago. She had no grandchildren. Johnny was her only flesh and blood. After returning home to read her letter, she flew from her home as swiftly as her 75 years would allow. She returned to the people in the Post Office and proudly announced that Johnny had apologized for being so tardy at letter writing. He gave her the most beautiful reason. He had married and they were now expecting a child. The best news of all, as soon as the baby was born they would be bringing the new daughter-in-law and grandchild to visit her.

Normally the catalogue orders took precedence over the regular mail. These were always strict necessities, and in many cases, a repair job may have been held up until the necessary tool arrived. But this was one exception where the regular mail had hit the jackpot and all thoughts of the catalogue orders were neglected as they savoured the news from Mrs. Smith.

THE LITTLE RED SCHOOL HOUSE

My formal years of school were spent in a one-room school house. There were from 16 to 24 pupils. Looking back I realize the teacher must have had her hands full with eight different classes and ages, some of whom were almost as old, and certainly as tall, as herself.

We walked one and a half miles each way. In summer it was nice but in the winter, in minus degree weather, it could become an ordeal. At times it was in the forty below range. Girls had no slacks and the boys wore knee high trousers. We wore hand knit socks, mitts, sweaters, toques and scarves, not to mention the long legged underwear. The scarves were made quite long to allow for wrapping around the face and ears. Even this was not enough to keep the bitter knife-like east wind from penetrating through the wool. We very often had to break a trail in new snow to get to the highway more than half a mile away. Roads were not ploughed, but if you were in luck, someone may have been out with a team of horses to break a path. Some of the families had a team of horses and their parents drove them. Our horses and Father spent every winter in the lumber camps so we were on our own as far as getting to school was concerned. We were fairly fortunate. My dad made us homemade skis and we could overcome the deep drifts this way.

There was no way you could send a six-year-old out in those conditions to battle the winter weather. Our education was a little delayed but people found their own solutions. It was generally accepted that beginners should start the school year at Easter and continue as late in the fall as possible. Most of us had frostbite or chilblains at one time or another. I had older brothers and sisters who coached me on the lessons of the day. I passed my entrance exams at twelve so I never suffered from not going to school in the winters.

A caretaker was hired, usually one of the older children, who was supposed to have a fire going and the place warmed up for us. Many times we arrived before he did, and had to struggle with starting a fire with hands that were paralysed from the cold. It took a long time to warm the room up as the door was constantly opening for more arrivals. Everyone crowded as close to the stove as possible. It took forever to heat the room. The ones next to the stove were quite comfortable, but the ones who had to sit in the far seats were never quite warm enough.

School was opened with the singing of God Save the Queen (or King), followed by the Lord's Prayer.

There were four rows of desks graduating from very small in front to normal sized at the back. The greatest humiliation for the older pupils was to be sent for punishment to sit in the tiny seats at the front where the teacher could keep an eye on them. They would have much preferred the strap.

On each desk was an ink well. The boys thought it great if the girl in front had long hair, to dip the end of the braids in the ink. We used slates until they were banished.

This school was divided, shortly after this picture was taken in 1912, into S. S #1 and S. S. #2 Victoria at Walford. Lena and Hazel are in the center of the front row. Lawrence is in the second row, third from the left.

Our first pens were the straight pen handles and you bought the nibs for them. We used a nib that was called "292". A beginner's tiny hands soon had the nibs jabbed into the paper and it took very little to destroy the nib. Pens were not allowed until Senior Second Grade. You considered yourself a big kid when you finally graduated to pen and ink.

Grades were Junior First, Senior First, Junior Second etc.; no such thing as kindergarten in our school. Not too many kids got as far as Senior Fourth and graduated. They were taken out of school as soon as they became old enough to be an extra hand at home.

The next item to replace the straight pen was the fountain pen. Oh, how marvellous to not have to dip into the ink well every three or four words! How embarrassing to have your pen run dry right in the middle of exams. You most likely got ink on your hands while filling it and it got on your exam papers. The ball point pen came out years after I left school. For our exams we used foolscap paper. It came in lined pads 8 ½ x 16 and was used only for examinations.

On Friday afternoons, when we didn't have my nemesis, Art, we would have spelling bees. Sometimes we had to see who could recite the times' tables. These contests were a lot of fun. I remember winning a five- cent notebook for a spelling contest. I thought it was just about the greatest thing that had ever happened to me.

We carried our lunches in shortening pails. The girls used the two pound size and the boys carried the five pound size. Our bread was always homemade. There was usually a cookie or cake, but there was very, very, seldom fresh fruit. No one grew fruit except for a few sour apples for pies. There was an abundance of wild fruit in the summer, which was always canned for use in the winter, but raw fruit was a real rarity.

One summer, in my early years, we had a great event in our school yard. Some of the earlier kids came to meet us and reported that a band of gypsies were camped in our school yard. We had heard of this but had never encountered it before. We were very excited, but nervous too. After all, didn't they steal kids and take them away? (Don't know why they would want us, as they had plenty of their own). These gypsy children, who came to meet us, were probably nervous too. The people were very friendly and we were enthralled with them. There were about five or six teams of horses. They had homemade canvas tops on the wagons. The people were darker skinned than we were used to. The children were scantily clothed but seemed to be having fun. They were just as curious about us as we were about them. They didn't stay long. This was the very last time they ever came and stayed. We never heard of them again and I often wonder where they went and what happened to them.

One of my favourite memories of school was the library. This was a cupboard on the wall about four feet square. Books were hard to come by. After our annual school concert, we decided how we would use the money. We usually bought some books over the protests of the non-readers. How we looked forward to the lists and selecting the books. Could you ever make a selection from the catalogue listings! If only you could have them all!

Throughout the school day, along with the pupils reciting was the screeching of slate pencils. I think it was only the first or second year at school that we used slates. Some of the older boys knew exactly how to make the most of the slate pencils to make a weird screeching noise.

I never went into a new class without a very good knowledge of what it entailed. When you had, the previous year, heard the lessons explained and recited, you absorbed much of it.

Our school did not supply the textbooks, and it was very hard for parents to come up with the money for books. They were handed down in the family but sometimes we were lucky to have some given to us from families when their children had no more need of them. In many cases we sat together and shared with ones who had none. I always loved school and never gave up learning. After I was married and our children were in school, I took night classes, then a course at our local College. I became a bookkeeper. This I loved, as figures and maths always fascinated me. Until I was 80, I kept taking more classes at the nearby High School.

I can still recite almost every piece of memory work we ever had. I just need someone to come up with a title and I can spiel it off. No wonder! We not only learned it, but heard the higher classes recite it, and when you were in a higher class, you heard the younger classes recite it.

Some teachers believed in the strap – spare the rod and spoil the child – but others managed nicely without. In our school, in my years, we never had a male teacher. Our Inspector was always a man and we were terrified, now I look back and wonder why. These men were mostly always kind to the teachers and to the pupils.

The younger children played hop scotch, tag, hide and seek, fox and the goose and many more. The older ones played mostly softball. Is it any wonder that I am a baseball addict still? Every year my grown up grandson takes me to the Sky Dome to see a game or two.

When I started school, it was just the one room with a couple of cloak rooms off the hall at the back. It must have been most nerve-wracking for the teacher on a bad weather day to have the kids' only play space right in the main room. There were the usual outhouses behind the school. They then built a woodshed, and the next year they made a full sized basement. That was a great place to play! There was nothing that could be damaged. There were many games of hockey played there.

Our Christmas concert was the only money-making project we ever had during the year. Of course there wasn't much money to spare if we had wanted more. Two or three weeks before the holidays we would decide what entertainment we were going to have; a couple of dialogues, a march formation, recitations, songs, perhaps a dance or pantomime, and a Christmas scene.

In the earlier days, we practised in recess and noon hours, but as the big night drew nearer, we spent the whole day honing our skills. We had to make costumes, which were improvised from whatever was handy. Horse- hair made a beautiful moustache for the boys and was always plentiful; sheets and flour bags were also easily acquired. The trees and the walls were decorated. There was a plentiful supply of greenery and we used quantities of spruce and cedar boughs. The smaller children made paper chains while the older children practised their lines.

The blackboards had every available space decorated with Christmas scenes. The artistic children drew theirs, but the non-talented like myself used stencils. Popcorn and cranberries were alternated on a thread to decorate the tree. All lead foil we could save from the coffee, tea and tobacco packages were used to cover cut out stars and angels which had already been cut out of heavy cardboard. These were proudly hung on the tree and pointed out to parents.

School was let out early on the last day and we went home to prepare for the highlight of our year. When we arrived, everything was, or seemed to be, chaos. The tension was almost unbearable. But finally one of the school trustees would speak the opening words and the concert began. Of course each one of us thought the part he or she was playing was most important. Parents proudly clapped and shouted at their favourites. As "Jingle Bells" rang out to the accompanying sleigh bells (there was no shortage of horse bells), Santa appeared and distributed a bag of candy for each child. Under the tree were the presents from the children, as we had drawn and exchanged names for gifts. These, from necessity, were mostly homemade. Most parents had some talent at which they excelled. The ladies might do a beautiful piece of needlework. My father was exceptionally talented and could come up with a great toy or game made from choice pieces of wood; that being the most plentiful thing on the farm. The children were clutching their precious bags of candies. In some cases this was the only candy they ever saw, and as for the others, very little more.

We drove to and from the school in sleighs, snuggling under the buffalo robes, in the frosty night air. The steam from our breath and the bright moonlight and shadows made it almost unreal as we went over the events of the evening. At home Mother made us hot chocolate. This was a rare, but welcome treat. It also helped us unwind from our gloriously exciting evening. Reluctantly we went off to bed convinced that never had there been a night so wonderful! It was the absolute high spot in our lives. And next Christmas was light years away, but not too far away for us to start planning for the next one.

MEMORABLE TEACHERS

When I was in my sixth grade at school, I had one teacher whom I have never forgotten. She was quite capable as a teacher but it was the other traits that I remember.

This teacher, I shall call her Miss M., was a neighbour of ours. She came from a very strict Catholic family. It was the lifetime dream of her parents that they have all of their children become either priests or nuns. Now that was just a bit unrealistic, as there were eleven children; one son became a priest (and in his mother's eyes a saint). The only fun loving, devil may care one of the family, became a nun. Only one of the family ever married. Miss M. had started out to be a nun but I can't remember just what happened that she never kept on, but she became a teaching Sister.

What changes we had to adapt. We were a one-room school house with about twenty boys and girls. The school house stood square in the centre of the yard. It became two separate playgrounds. The west side became the boys' side and the east side was the girls'. Definitely no mixing! There was a line, invisible, but very, very powerful. We were unable to have a ball game, a decent hockey game or anything else that required a fixed number of players. There were quite a few small children who were too small to join in the games.

We had no indoor plumbing, just the outhouses. We swore no one had ever seen our teacher visit one, and as she never went home for lunch, we decided that she wasn't built like the rest of us and had no bodily functions. Perhaps that explained her weird ideas.

Inside, it was again, boys one side and girls on the other. When we were called up to the front for our lessons, the same procedure was applied. She had us form two groups. Heaven help the kid who was caught smuggling a note across the aisle, especially if it was the opposite sex.

We liked Miss M. as she was very kind to us, but she surely took the fun out of our lives apart from school hours. So of course the kids (boys mostly) thought up tricks to get even. Their tricks were mostly harmless but annoying. She was an excellent teacher, and kept good order.

When four o'clock came, she stood at the door and sent the girls off first. When they were well down the road she then let the boys leave. Little did she know that we waited just out of sight until the boys caught up to us. We started coming earlier to school to have a quick game of ball, but Miss M., as soon as she found out, came earlier also.

Her lessons were edited from the textbooks. It is surprising how many things take on a different meaning when you have a pure mind. Well she tried her best but was not always successful in imparting her version to us. We took a delight in doing our assignments from the original version, only to be reprimanded and punished for it.

The one outstanding thing I remember, is the day someone's cat came to school. It behaved beautifully and was petted and made much of. We were having a hygiene lesson not long before closing time. Miss M. was explaining that everything we ate that was not used up in energy, turned to blood. Well that cat was not going to let her off with that. Just about then he tried to dig a hole with no success so just did what he had to do right there. The whole school room was in hysterics by then, but poor Miss M. just wanted to crawl away and hide!

The year that I went into eighth grade we had a terrible teacher. I had skipped Grade Seven and was looking forward to trying my entrance that year.

Miss B. was the most useless person I could ever imagine. She taught nothing and kept no order. The kids just roved around and did as they pleased. Many times I have seen the boys going from one end of the school to the other on top of the desks; and this in school hours! Anyone passing by on the road could see, at any time, two or three heads standing, gazing out. I can never imagine how she ever passed her exams for teaching. This was not her first school, but it was her last.

By Christmas time, the school board had decided, after repeated warnings, that enough was enough. When school started in January, we had a new teacher.

As she walked up the aisle, we all looked around to get a peek. She clipped one young lad on the ear and said: "Eyes front, young man." And believe me, all eyes turned front.

Our halcyon days were over. She was very strict. But how she could teach! I think if I could wish for something nice for all children, it would be for them to have a teacher like Miss S.

She had a double load as she had to do a full year's work in half a year. She was equal to the task. Once the children knew they couldn't fool around, there was no problem. They never tried her out, because they knew they would come out the losers.

There were seven of us in the entrance class, a large one for that school. To help make up for lost time, she kept our class in for fifteen or twenty minutes some evenings, and sometimes a few minutes of our lunch hour.

Miss S. always treated us as adults, and expected our best. She mostly received it from us.

Near the end of the season, just a couple of weeks before exam time, she and I were waiting for the others to show up. I will never know where I found the nerve to ask her what had been puzzling me for some time. When my mother found out what I had done, she was horrified. I asked Miss S. why, being such an excellent teacher, was she free to come to us. Miss S. seemed pleased at my question. She was 27 at the time. She had a school for September, she explained, but had taken pneumonia and then rheumatic fever. She was ill all that fall, and of course they had to replace her. Their loss but our gain.

HALLOWE'EN

Fall was a very busy time of year for us. There was the entire crop of vegetables to gather. The turnip crop was the last. It would be cold and frosty and our hands were nearly frozen when we worked with the turnips. While our hands were freezing, we talked and planned for Hallowe'en. Sometimes we would finish the turnips on that day. Some of the nastier plans were reluctantly discarded.

One Hallowe'en I can remember, we worked in six inches of snow. Our gloves were soon soaked and freezing. But through it all we made our plans. We often exchanged help with the neighbours and for weeks there was plotting and planning on our new Hallowe'en pranks. This was a great opportunity to discuss our plans without danger of the adults hearing. We would walk up and down the rows pulling and trimming the turnips and devising our strategies for this year.

There was usually a party somewhere. Some neighbours were a bit dubious about lending their homes as they didn't always trust us in the line of pranks. Mostly we spared the host and hostess, but there was very often one who didn't play by our rules. The younger kids played their pranks earlier in the evening but the older ones went out after the party. We had not yet heard of "Trick or Treat". A couple of families didn't believe in dancing and their children weren't allowed to come to the dance. The kids resented this and often played their own pranks while the party was on. The night of our party there were fence rails piled high across our side road.

One year a startled housewife found a strange rooster in her hen house. After having no luck at finding out who was the true owner, she decided that some Sunday when she had company, it would make a great stew.

Some pranks were just for a laugh, but they often got carried away and got out of hand.

One year, some of the teenage boys, my brothers included, took a wagon apart and put it on the roof peak of an old log cabin. There they assembled it together again. The owner of the wagon was not too happy. He had no family of his own and didn't know how he would retrieve it. After a week or so, (with some less than gentle persuasion from the parents) the boys went one night and brought it down and assembled it again. The boys classified this as getting even: the gentleman in question had a strong pair of field glasses and was not shy in using them. Sometimes when we got home from school, our parents knew everything that went on with us the whole way home. Mr. --- and his wife would call up our home and say, "Jack, or Cliff, was fighting with Dick, or Mike" on the way home from school. It was very often not a fight but a wrestling match. They had, from where they lived, a good view of the road right to the school house. We didn't like this very well, especially as the adult was always right. We were never allowed to defend ourselves. The adults had spoken and that was that! Most Hallowe'ens found us doing a few pranks on this couple, but none as drastic as the wagon. One night we caught a couple of his hens and shut them in the outdoor john. Mr. --- had quite a fright when he went out in the middle of the night. We never did find out if he made it in time after his fright. Another prank was to move the outhouse back by about two or three feet.

One year my mother was approached to see if she would host the Hallowe'en party that year. She agreed, as she had hosted it on other occasions. Our very small house could always expand to make room for the visitors. It was the custom for everyone to bring some food. A couple of the bachelor boys brought Mom some chickens that evening for her to cook. They roasted in the oven while the party was in progress and almost drove us crazy with the delicious aromas. Chicken was not nearly as commonplace then as it is now, and we thought they were quite generous and thoughtful. It was a great party with fond memories; that is until a few weeks later, when Mom found out that the chickens had been stolen from someone else's hen house early in the evening as a Hallowe'en trick. The pranksters had found a lonely spot, built a bonfire and dressed the birds with the help of a few others before bringing them to us. My mom really exploded as she felt that she had been used. She was known for her honesty and integrity. It just went against the grain to know she had been cooking and serving stolen goods. Most of the people could ill afford the loss of the poultry.

Next year another lady was asked to do the honours. She made it perfectly clear that she would be no party to stolen goods. The men solved the problem and showed their good faith by bringing them to the lady the day before Hallowe'en. That sounded fair. They were definitely not a Hallowe'en prank, or so they said. It was a year later that the lady found out that the chickens were stolen a night early. The lady was as enraged as my mom had been. The people from whom the birds had been stolen sat up all Hallowe'en night with a shot gun and a dog while their birds were roasting tantalizingly in the lady's oven. Needless to say, this was the end of the Hallowe'en dances for quite a few years. The only redeeming thing about it was that they had been taken, this time, from a very well-to-do farmer; the one with the field glasses. He had made trouble for most of the ones who were in on the prank and they felt that they were justly entitled to score one on him.

In the twenties, there were few cars. Everyone relied on living horse power. A man's pride and joy were his horses. Some could afford very showy well-bred ones, but most of us had just what we could afford. Still, whatever horses a man owned, they were quite special to him.

One Hallowe'en night an exchange was made that gave us a laugh for years to come. One very proud farmer had a pair of quite well-bred horses. They were very high steppers, too well-bred for heavy farm work. Much like using a Cadillac for trucking. One other farmer had a pair of horses that were about as poor as you could get. One year the day after Hallowe'en, Mr. B., with the high steppers, went out to do his chores. Upon entering the stable he let out a sonic sized bellow for there beside his one beauty was a ragged, scruffy animal dying of the heaves!

COUNTRY FALL FAIRS

Did you ever, as a child, attend a country fair? Do you remember the mind-boggling smells, sights and sounds, each striving to outdo the others? To a young child who has never been away from home, it was holiday time, Christmas, and July 1, all wrapped up together.

The Massey Fair was a one day affair packed with a year's worth of excitement. For us it began the day before when we prepared the vegetables that were to be shown. They were graded as to colour, shape, and matching size, then scrubbed and cleaned. The animals received the same brushing and cleaning attention.

Mother had pickles, preserves, and jams, which had been made some time before. The house was full of yummy smells from the baking that was going to be shown the next day. I have forgotten the individual things Mom made, but I do remember the activity and excitement. I couldn't imagine anyone else could enter better things than what my mother was making.

The day of the fair began for us at 4 a.m.; chores had to be done, breakfast had to be prepared and eaten, and the livestock we were taking had to be made ready. We had a purebred Hereford bull that won many prizes. Dad, or one of my brothers, walked him the twelve miles there and back. A special calf, pig, or sheep would have to ride with us in the wagon.

When we arrived of course we all wanted to see everything at once. The boys went off together while we followed our mother.

It was a small fair then and the entries were judged in the morning and ready for showing by one o'clock. What pushing and juggling for a good spot when the door opened to let us in! It seemed we could hardly see if our entries had won the coveted red ribbon, and how disappointing when we found we only had won some of them.

What eye catching, mouth watering things for us; the luscious rainbow coloured rows of jams, red raspberries, strawberries and cherries, purple grapes and damson plums, and yellow gooseberries and plums. Then there were the pickles and canned vegetables, just as eye exciting but not quite as interesting as the sweets. The breath stoppers were: pastries two or three inches deep, with luscious juice dribbling from the small cut piece which was used by the judges to decide the winner; and cakes six inches high with an inch of icing between the layers, or so it seemed to us little ones. Certainly Mother's never looked quite that way at home. And then there were the cookies, raisin and nut-filled delicacies, large and fat, much nicer and more tempting than the small dainty tea ones. Each item had one small piece removed for judging but how, oh how, could a judge ever decide on looks alone? They (the judges) must be made of sawdust not to have sampled each one as it stood in all its glory. There were tarts of every description, bread, buns, tea biscuits, enough to drive you crazy.

The boys had their own brand of exciting moments. There were the vegetable and grain exhibits. Then there were the animals, horses, cattle, pigs, sheep, some goats, and

Jim Thom and son Cliff at School Fair.

Verna's brother Cliff and Hereford calf at School Fair.

the poultry exhibits. The smell of manure mixed with taffy apples, popcorn, and candyfloss were part of the fair, as was the band music and blaring loudspeakers.

There were races and ball games for the kids and there were a few horse races. The boys made exciting new friends and renewed acquaintances from other years.

Mother had packed plenty of food for a picnic lunch at noon. There was enough for another meal before we started back home. I can remember us coming home after dark, tired and sleepy, but we all had to turn out for chores before we could go to bed.

Jim and Verna on their wedding day, September 28, 1942.

Another fair on a smaller level, but more personal, was our school fair. In the spring, the school board issued us seeds to be planted and later shown at our fair. There was a list of vegetables and flowers with descriptions of each. We brought the list home. The whole family took part in deciding what we would choose for our exhibits.

We always had stock to show. Our brothers picked the likeliest calves and had them well halter broken. The girls baked and sewed. We were in contest with another larger school. We entered artwork and writing. Believe me, I never won anything in artwork, but I had prizes for handwriting, knitting, collections and baking. We made collections of dried and pressed leaves, insects and samples of different woods. We had races and a ball game.

At about four thirty we gathered at the hall where we were given our prize money and received the news of which school had won the most points. What jubilation and rejoicing when we discovered we had won! Of course our school didn't win every year, but it was worth it when we did. The other school had twice as many pupils as ours.

As an adult I still love to go to fairs and I never enter the grounds that I don't recall all the thrills and excitement I experienced as a child. Now the Massey Fair can hold its own with any other country fair. It is three days instead of one. I love to go back every few years, meet old friends and just reminisce.

I married a farmer. He was six feet tall and very slight. But he had a tremendous appetite. He liked everything I made. It was a delight to cook and bake because it was greatly appreciated. Some twenty years later I became an exhibitor myself. I entered baking, jams, jellies and knitting. One day when I was being congratulated on my prizes by a former boarder at our home, an old neighbour and friend retorted, "Take a good look at that husband of hers and you would swear that he never ate a square meal in his life."

EMPLOYMENT

We, in our community, were all farmers. Even though we had 160 acres, there were few tillable acres. Each farm was one half mile by one half mile. There were probably 50 acres of rock on each farm and many more acres of bush. Clearing land was a long, slow, laborious job, needing many, many hours, days and weeks for a single acre. It also needed a farmer with a few strong sons.

First of all the trees had to be cut down. We used wood to cook and heat our homes so this was most useful. The limbs and trimmings from the trees had to be piled in neat stacks (brush piles) and left to dry. After the stove wood was hauled away, the stumps had to be left for at least a year to dry and the roots to die. When a sufficient time had elapsed for the clearing to begin, as many roots as possible were chopped off close to the stump. A chain was fastened around the root and a horse was used to haul this free. In most cases it took many tries. A shovel and pick were used to dig down a little more and clear the secondary roots. One man and a horse could work a whole afternoon on just a couple of trees. Sometimes brush piles were piled onto the tree stump and burned to destroy as much as possible before attacking the tree. When all the tree stumps had been cleared, they were piled in heaps to dry and later burned. Some were piled in windrows for a make-do temporary fence.

In the part of the country where we lived, stones and rocks were most prevalent. Some of the stones were heartbreakers. Even after a year or two when you thought you had them all cleared, they crept to the surface. Some of my nice memories are of riding on a stone boat, which was a sort of sledge. In later years, I had to help pile the stones on and it was not quite so much fun. It was a matter of course that the stone boat was taken to the fields when they were being cultivated. In many cases the stones were manageable, but sometimes one could be larger. If one caught on the cutting bar of the mower or other machinery, it could do any amount of damage.

In some areas where a man didn't own a farm, he hired out to a farmer to clear land. He might have some grown sons to help him. Most farmers did not have the money to pay for this service. The wages could very often be negotiated in trade. During the depression, this service was often offered for their board. It was no joke to put food on the table for a number of hungry men. It was very rare that any of the farmers could offer the job of clearing land.

The number of cleared acres could not keep a family completely so there was always the search for a little more income. A little job here and another one there was greatly appreciated. There was no such thing as a full time job; at least not in the area where I was raised. A bachelor, if offered a job of land clearing, would work for little more than his board. He appreciated the good food after trying to fend for himself.

The most consistent jobs were the lumber camps in the winter time. Farmers for miles around were hired. Their teams were hired also. This was for the months of January, February and part of March.

For many years the employers were the J. J. McFadden Lumber Company. It was personal to us as two of my sisters-in-law worked as maids in the J. J. McFadden household. He had a great interest in farming. On his visits to my father-in-law's farm to pick up one of the girls, he promised my husband a horse for a wedding present when and if he married. A few months after we were married and were starting to farm, Jim wrote to him and received a very gracious answer. He could go to the horse barns at Blind River and have his pick of twenty horses. Who else can say they had a horse given them for a wedding present? (Of course it was not gift wrapped)!

All the previous fall, at the camps, there had been a crew cutting trees and getting them ready to haul to the river, then later to be floated down the Mississauga to the mill at Blind River.

The Lumber Company had quite a number of their own horses as well as the farm teams they hired for the winter. Wages were not large, but men and teams were fed and sheltered. It was greatly appreciated that more stock could be kept over winter on the farm when there was no team to feed for a few months. Someone complained to J. J. McFadden that a certain person was not pulling his weight around the camp. "I guess," J. J. replied, "I can afford to feed him much easier than his parents can."

Jim at the Lumber Camp. The horse in front was received as a wedding present.

Trails were swamped out and iced from the huge piles of logs awaiting delivery to the river. There they were piled on the ice to stay until the spring break up. It was a mind-boggling sight to see how much could be transported in a single load with the help of the "crazy wheel". There was one team that did nothing else, but drive the water cart and ice the roads. Once the team got the sleigh moving and on the down hill run, it was just a matter of the horses keeping out of the way, for that load went down the skid way like greased lightning. This was where the "crazy wheel" came into use, in slowing the process. All horses had to have very sharp shoes.

When the break up came in the spring, there was great excitement and activity. Boom logs were established at all crucial points. A creek flowing into the river was boomed, as were the bays where the logs might pile up.

A bunk house and cook shack were erected on a raft of logs. Men with peavies, cant hooks, axes, and other tools, rode the logs and kept them from piling. A log jam was a very serious event. The longer it took to clear it, the larger the pile-up. Clearing a log jam took an abundance of nerve and plenty of "know-how" to find the key log and move it. Sometimes the only way to dislodge the jam was to use dynamite. This was used only as a last resort. Many men have lost their lives on the spring drive breaking up log jams.

My father didn't like the bush work. He preferred the job of toting. This consisted of hauling supplies from Iron Bridge to the camps. All supplies were dependent on horses and sleighs for transportation to the camp. This was a most uncomfortable and cold

Picture taken at the Lumber Camp. Jim is on left in back row (with beard).

journey. I am not sure how long it took for one return trip. I do know there was a halfway house, and probably more stopovers. We had a pair of roan horses that were famous for their stamina for many miles around. They were not a very large team but everyone knew Bob and Roy. They were badly spoiled by all the crew at the camp. Both horses loved tobacco, bread and cookies; in fact anything that the men fed them. My dad worked in camp every winter. He worked there the year he was seventy and then he decided he would retire.

When the men came home from the lumber camp, the money was used for seed grain, and all the things we had needed and done without all winter. There was usually a grocery bill, as most cows were not milking and the hens didn't lay in the winter. Calves were usually born in the spring, so the cows were in their dry period in the winter. The hens took this time to rest also. We couldn't afford the extra feed it would have taken to make them lay. The first egg of spring was a big event. In the fall before they stopped laying, we would lay a supply away in water glass, a solution that would keep them for quite awhile.

In the fall, when we had a little money, we used to order from the ads in the farm papers, a large supply of honey, jam and peanut butter. I can just drool when I think of a big thick crust of crunchy fresh bread and fresh honey, and sitting around the kitchen stove to enjoy it.

Our taxes were very little and we had what they called dollar-for- dollar. If your taxes were a fixed amount, they allowed you to work it off in road work plus the same amount you did for free. That is if we put in a few days for free to work off our taxes, we could work the same number of days and get paid for it. We had a half-mile of side road, so that is where our work went. If you needed more to keep up the road, you traded time with your neighbours.

Some years we were lucky enough to have a road grant in our area. If so, one or more of the men would apply. No more than one person per family was allowed. Wages were one dollar a day for a man and the same for a team of horses. One of our neighbours showed up at the job site hoping to be hired with his team. The foreman, being a bit snooty said, "Kind of light harness you have there." "Kind of light wages you are paying" was the reply he received.

During the worst part of the depression, the Government was trying to find ways to keep people off the relief rolls. In our community, almost everyone was on relief. Our family was just as hard up as anyone else but refused to accept help. I suppose that was the old Scottish pride showing. There were only two other families, beside ourselves, who weren't on the dole. That made it extra hard for us. Every month after the relief cheque came in, our peers came decked out in new shoes, coats, dresses, etc., all purchased from the catalogues. We were still wearing our old patched hand-me-down clothes. This was in the era when I was wearing my brother's shoes.

It was in 1938 that the Government gave a grant to redo highway 17 from Spanish to Cutler, a distance of about five miles. Men were hired from the surrounding areas. They were receiving the grand sum of thirty dollars per month, plus room and board. The farmers who hired out their teams received an extra dollar per day for their teams. The work started in April and continued until about July 1. Most of the farmers had to leave anyway and get the hay crop in. My husband-to-be had his dad's team there but he had to go home for the haying. My brother Cliff had our team there and also had to go home. The Government had a wee bit more to spend so they kept on a skeleton crew. My brother Jack stayed on. The crew received the magnificent sum of $5.00 per month as wages. Of course they received their board, but if they missed a day on account of sickness, they were docked the equivalent of a days work. One man received a cheque for four cents.

Few summers passed without one or two forest fires that got out of hand and had to be fought with as many men as were available. We hated how the money was earned, but were grateful for the cash received for it.

Every farmer had a large supply of trees, and all heated their homes and cooked with wood stoves. The village people had no such source so they were forced to buy their wood. However, those people who lived near the Spanish River spent a lot of their time hauling out driftwood and the logs that had escaped the river drives. There were river drives on the Spanish, but not to the same extent as the Mississauga drive.

Our men spent whatever time they could spare cutting stove wood. We usually supplied the school house. We had different customers that we sold to quite frequently. In Spanish, there was Tim Kelly's Bake Shop and a boarding school for Indian girls. They bought huge supplies of firewood.

There was always a bit of trapping. During the depression it was hard to sell furs. I suppose they also had problems getting buyers. We caught a few weasels, which were devils to have around. Their pelts, though small, were worth good money. Weasels, however, are blood thirsty and vicious. It is a very small animal, not much larger than a rat, but will tackle a rabbit three times its size. It can get into a hen house through a hole hardly big enough for a mosquito, and slaughter every bird in there. We have many times been cleaned right out of poultry by one weasel in one night. They go for the throat, and just keep on killing. We never had any qualms about trapping weasels.

Foxes were easy to trap. Don't let the term "foxy" mislead you. They aren't that smart.

In springtime floods, there were always muskrats to trap. At this time beavers were so scarce they were almost extinct so no beaver could be caught.

If I make light of a fox's intelligence, I make it up when I mention coyotes. The wily old coyote is an apt description, but too tame. They have all the intelligence of ten ordinary animals, plus an almost human thought process. I could fill pages just telling how they outwitted would-be trappers. They were high on our list for trapping, as even just one captured was money in hand. A coyote could be a nuisance if you kept sheep. Some ate more mutton off us than we did. They could clean up chickens and turkeys in a hurry, or anything else that tempted them. The hide was worth only a couple of dollars; not much, but still good when sometimes you never saw any cash money from fall till spring. The reason they were so sought after was the $25.00 bounty the Government gave us for each one trapped or shot. This was almost as much money as a man could earn in a month.

They could smell a human so easily. Traps were boiled in a tub of water and then left over a smoking fire to erase the human odour. Gloves and boots were smoked over the same fire and used to handle the traps. At this stage, the traps were never handled by bare hands. The trappers would stomp their boots in the ashes. Traps were set on coyote trails, then covered very carefully with twigs or leaves, or whatever was there naturally. Next day when you went to check the traps, you might very well find them overturned and urinated on. They left you the message, "You will have to do better than that the next time"! They seemed to have their own sense of humour. One time after capturing one alive, Dad tied it up outside overnight. Mother raised the roof until he did what he should have done earlier. During the night, another coyote had come within a short distance of the buildings. Tracks were all around, although we hadn't heard a thing.

I remember my brother coming home in a storm at ten o'clock at night. On our side road a coyote had just crossed the road ahead of him. The tracks were filling up with snow almost as soon as they were made. These hadn't even started to fill in. He and Dad got some traps and went down with the lantern and set them just where the animal had crossed the fence. Next morning we had one trapped. That was the easiest one we ever trapped. There was so much snow covering the scent and the traps, that they weren't alarmed.

We always tried to grow extra potatoes and turnips for sale. One of our men would load up bags of vegetables and take them into the village. If the housewives had a bit of cash, they loved to buy this way as it was much cheaper. Sometimes we had someone come in from another town to buy up extra potatoes. That caused a lot of excitement, as many families could sell as many as fifty bags and this brought the cash that was so badly needed. We had very little sale for vegetables. Most of the people in our village grew their own gardens. Some, of course, were older, or they hadn't planted enough to see them through. When an order for potatoes came in, it meant a boxcar load. Potatoes were always sold in hundred weight bags.

When we were kids we sometimes could find sale for pine cones. The pines were being cut at a terrific rate. In the late twenties, the Government began to take notice and they tried re-seeding. Teenage lads were hired for a couple of summers, but by then the depression had caught up with us and they didn't continue the program.

Before an election was our very best time for employment. The present government had to show that it was making employment for everyone, and hoped that the lean times would be conveniently overlooked. This was when we might get a road grant.

For women, the choices were few; house work and house work. Most of the girls had not even made it through Grade Eight, and even if they had, there was nothing else. When a new baby was expected, a young girl was usually hired for a month. It was all most families could afford. Girls usually made fifteen dollars a month.

During the thirties, a Tourist Resort was started a few miles from us. This should have created jobs for a few people, but the family had many relatives, so few extras were needed. My sister did get a few weeks of work there for about two dollars a week and her board. Their own daughters received no wages, but were put in the areas where tips were received. Their jobs brought in more money than the paid ones.

Once World War II started up, jobs were plentiful, and girls could find jobs anywhere, though the wage scale had not improved. I worked once in a restaurant in Sault Ste. Marie. It was open 24 hours per day. There were two shifts, 7:00 a.m. to 7:00 p.m. We had no days off and received ten dollars a week plus our board. I worked 84 hours a week for eight months. Definitely not union hours!

ENTERTAINMENT

How do you have fun when you and your peers have absolutely not a penny? The key to this is that none of you have any money.

One of my favourite entertainments was softball. Saturday was an extra busy day on the farm. There was the whole house to clean and a generous supply of baking was needed, which also included bread. There was usually company on Sunday, sometimes unexpected. You may have been tired in the late afternoon, but when supper was over and the chores were done, the energy started to flow and you could forget that you had done, not only a full day's work, but a whole week of hard slugging work.

Everyone gathered at the school yard, including teens and older ones. We used the school bat and balls. If a ball wore out, those who had money donated a penny or two and soon we had the fifteen or twenty cents it took to buy a new one.

We had picnics. This was the best of all the ways of visiting. Everyone was welcome. There was the Orange Day, July 12; the United Farmers of Ontario; the first of July; and of course the family picnics. Our family was scattered from Sudbury to the Soo. We were nearly half way for all to gather. Everyone contributed food. It was an awesome sight to our unsophisticated eyes to see those tables spread with each family's donations.

We saw foods, at times like these, that we had never even seen let alone eaten. So that was what a watermelon looked like! Grapes, peppers and even celery were quite unknown to us. We always thought that if you didn't grow it, you didn't eat it. Sometimes someone turned up with a freezer of ice cream. Now that was something else! We only had about one family picnic a year, and the people were never the same, so it was always something which we anticipated with great excitement.

In the winter, on Saturday evenings, someone would graciously offer her home for a dance. No invitations were given as everyone was welcome. The party line telephone took care of letting people know where and when it was taking place. The music was guitar, piano, violin or whatever was available. It might even be a mouth organ.

We all brought lunch which was served at midnight, then it was back to dancing for another hour or two. We would have two or three of these dances per month.

A winter favourite was the sleigh ride. The word circulated that there was a team and sleigh available. The sleigh bed was covered with a foot or so of sweet smelling hay and covered with buffalo or other robes. The current boy friend slipped over beside you and more robes were used to cover you up. You snuggled up under the covers, with very often a beautiful full moon turning the snow to a fairyland. My goodness it was cozy, but what funny things happened under those robes!

We had skating parties. If you didn't own skates, you went anyway. I never had a decent pair of skates, just an old pair strapped onto a pair of shoes. In any case, a good pair of skates would have been wasted as I was hopeless on skates. However, I excelled on skis. We also had sleigh and toboggan parties. The toboggans were sometimes just cardboard boxes or large pieces of tin, or just anything a person could use to slide down the hill; the more tumbles the better. Because my father was so handy, we had homemade sleighs which held a packed six or eight. Lunch was made by each of us and given to our hostess, who usually served us hot cocoa, and didn't it taste good!

When I was in my teens, we girls started a knitting club, which met during the winter months, and it became very popular. Imagine my surprise just recently, when I was at a funeral in my old home town when two strange men asked me if I still did any knitting. Knitting and crocheting were my favourite hobbies and I wondered if they were mind readers. I was open- mouthed until they introduced themselves. They were some of my old friends I hadn't seen in over fifty years.

At home in the evenings, we very often had to work. The younger ones would wind yarn, made from our own sheep's wool. With all of the women knitting, we went through an enormous amount of wool. The women knitted and mended. Mother made quilts. Dad would be whittling or making some item; the boys would probably be mending harness. When we did have free evenings, we played cards or crocinole. This was in the winter time.

We knit socks to the knee, for men and women. There were also toques, scarves and sweaters.

In the winter we would have a dance in one of the halls, and have a Box Social at midnight. This was a special event that we only had about once a year. What planning and scheming went into that! If you had a regular boyfriend, you gave him a clue as to how your box would be decorated. Heaven help him if he bought a box belonging to another girl, because you ate with the one who brought the box. There was a lot of good natured fun seeing who could bring the best decorated box. In some cases the contents didn't live up to the fancy exterior. There was the odd lousy cook around.

Sometimes this worked in reverse. If you had someone vying for your favours, and he was not your choice, you had to trick him and pull the wool over his eyes. He might try to bribe a younger sister, brother or a girl friend to say what your box might look like. If you had any idea before hand this was going to happen, you took precautions and had the informants give misleading information. To his chagrin, he found himself buying a box that belonged to someone he didn't care for.

A box would contain sandwiches, pickles, cheese, cookies, cake or pie. We didn't have too many extras, but it was amazing how much variety was put into it.

These socials were attended by everyone, young and old. Many a misguided suitor found himself sharing a box with a sixty-year-old lady, or the reverse side of the coin. I never had to share mine with a sixty-year-old man. Guess I was just lucky. Now, at my age, a sixty-year-old looks pretty young!

In the summer we played ball or horse shoes, or any of the many things we found to do. We all loved to read but didn't have too much reading material. We had the weekly Family Herald and the twice weekly Ottawa Farm Journal. These were read from cover to cover. In the first year of our married life on the farm, the Ottawa Journal offered a pure bred pig for getting a certain number of subscriptions. I won one and the next year I earned another. This began the pure bred line of pigs we had over the years.

The helping "bees" were always a social event. There was the wood cutting bee in the winter. A neighbour woman or two would come over that day and help. It was a good excuse for a visit, and of course the men did their own socializing. The bee was always preceded by a very busy day cooking and baking. With sometimes not too much variety, it took a lot of ingenuity to come up with wholesome and appetizing meals. My mother was a real whiz at making the most out of very little and what she did was excellent.

We had threshing bees in the late summer. This was much busier for us as we had about twelve or fourteen men as compared to the eight or ten for the woodcutting. It took a large amount of baking to serve so many men for two or three meals. Dad sometimes slaughtered a lamb.

After we were married and living in Southern Ontario there was one special bee in Greenbank for us. Three of our family of four were just out of hospital recovering from a very serious car accident. Our twelve-year-old son was the only one not hurt. We had only come home the day before, and were still in pretty bad shape, when tractors began pulling into the yard. Some of the men left food at the door. When we inquired what was going on, they told us they were filling our corn silo. It was a few days earlier than was usual, but they felt we would recover better if the silo was filled and we wouldn't have to worry about how we would manage by ourselves. The women came in later, put me back to bed and took over the kitchen. They set up tables outside and fed the men out there so as not to disturb me. What a helpless feeling to know that there was so much to be done and I was either in bed or had my head over the toilet throwing up nothing. What beautiful neighbours! The best part of it was that they did it willingly and thoroughly enjoyed doing it.

Mother usually had at least one quilt ready for quilting. There was a group of about six women who lived near each other and were considered good quilters. As each one had a quilt to do each winter there was socializing there. An invitation to a quilting was much prized. It meant a whole day out, someone else's cooking, meeting your friends and the special pride when you knew they valued your quilting ability.

Then there were the barn building bees, almost before my time, but I did see a few where they were raising an auxiliary building. This was really a neighbourhood project at the time of raising. My dad built the framework of some of them, and sometimes it was done by a pair of them. Planning started more than a year in advance. The timber had to be felled and dried. That at least was plentiful. They could afford to be picky and use only the very best. The logs were examined closely to see if they were dried enough and if they were straight and true. They were measured carefully and the adze was used to square them. Each side of the barn was built and laid out on the ground, then the rafters were cut.

The day of the raising, the sections were held together until they had a framework up. By late afternoon they were putting on the roof, invariably shingles or shakes. Sometimes, these were hand done. If the farmer had a few sons at home, they could probably make all their own shingles. The others took their cedar to the mill and had them done. There would be from 20 to 60 men at a barn raising, depending on the weather, the time of the year, how well liked the farmer was, and many other factors. Most liked to have a raising in the spring so the new crop could be stored. This of course had to be worked around seeding, etc.

It was not an easy time for women either. Those were the days of the old wood cook stove with ovens that held one cake or four loaves of bread. There being no electricity, the perishables had to be held as late as possible.

No woman ever came to a barn raising empty handed. She brought at least a couple of items. There were bean salads, potato salads, pickles, hard boiled eggs, pies, cakes, cookies or even sauerkraut. Each person had her own specialty.

The lady of the house was responsible for putting it all together. It was a giant pot luck, but she had a pretty good idea of who would bring what. She would have the meat to cook. It would be roast beef, pork or lamb, fish and chicken. Some of these would be cold as the oven was overworked. She also had all the vegetables to prepare and cook. Sometimes there was an outside fire made to take care of the overflow. Everything was cooked in oversized pots, many of them borrowed. Long trestle tables were set up outside made from the unending supply of lumber and sawhorses. The tables were covered with newspaper and topped with a white tablecloth or white sheets if needed. Benches were made of lumber and wood blocks.

Dishes were borrowed from the nearest neighbours. There was a never ending supply of dishes to be washed. The young people, who were too young to cook, were kept busy carrying water and heating it or doing all the odd jobs that accumulated. When the men had been fed, the ladies had their turn. When they had eaten, it was time to begin preparing for supper.

When supper was over the chores had to be done. Some of the men had to go home for chores but they would be back. The men who weren't choring continued on the barn. It was all done except the floor. That must be finished before the next event – the big event of the day – happened. It was the barn raising dance, sometimes called the hell raising dance. Anyone who had a musical instrument brought it. There were violins, guitars, and accordions for sure. The dancing kept up for hours. Everyone was fed again.

At about two in the morning people began leaving. Many of them lived some distance away and were travelling by wagons or buggies. As most of the people had been up at 4:00 that morning to have chores done, and had chores to be done again an hour or so after they arrived home, you can imagine what a tough breed of people we had. No unions striking for a thirty hour week in those days.

COMMUNICATIONS

In the twenties and thirties there were many ways of communicating. There were telegrams, telephones, word of mouth and the mail. The mail in the early years of the twentieth century was most commendable. We now have computers, fax and E-mail. In spite of these modern and faster (Ouch!) gadgets, the mail has gone the way of the buffalo with the speed of a tortoise.

The C.P.R. had a spur line from Sudbury to the Soo. This serviced us quite adequately. In the morning there was the West bound local arriving at Walford, our local village, at around 8:00 in the morning and in the Soo shortly before noon. It left the Soo about 4:00 p.m. and was at Walford by 7:30. Our village was 120 miles from the Soo. We could, if we had business there, make the return trip in the same day.

Then, in the afternoon, there was #17 Westbound, and #18 Eastbound, two or three hours later.

It now takes a week to receive a letter from Toronto to Oshawa (thirty miles) if you are lucky. In our youth we could send a letter to the Soo on the morning local. In the main part of town, there was delivery twice a day. Since there was no junk mail, it didn't take long. If you received something that necessitated an answer, you wrote your answer and it could be taken to the main Post Office where it would find its way onto the evening local. The mail was sorted after each train. If the person went to the Post Office after the evening local there was your answer.

When we moved to Southern Ontario, I would write to my mother on Monday and receive an answer on Wednesday.

As a child I can never remember when we didn't have a telephone. We were very poor and to us, the phone was a great luxury. It was installed in 1919. We had over thirty subscribers, and all had their own individual longs and shorts. It didn't take long to memorize the series of rings. Ours was four long and five short ones. There were very few social times in our lives, so any ring of the telephone could spark a little excitement. Each call rang in every home.

The telephone was a box on the wall. It had two large bells. There was a handle on the side to crank out your calls. To place a call out of our area, you pressed a button on the side and made one long ring, which alerted the operator. She then placed your call. There were very few long distance calls, except in an emergency; probably for a doctor.

The cost was about $5.00 dollars a year. Someone who had a bit of technical ability was hired to repair the phone when something went wrong. There were not too many things to go wrong; it was probably the batteries. Each phone had two large batteries, which would get weaker as time went on. The "listening queens", of course, were way up there in the lead for replacements. The cost of the batteries was included in the annual charges.

Before using the phone, we would lift the receiver and ask "Using?" Imagine going to the phone and before you could speak, you heard your name in discussion. That would surely make an eavesdropper of you if only for a few minutes.

The phone had various uses, and was a great source of gossip. Many never missed a ring, and because it was an open line it was there for all. One time my mother was visiting a friend, who was a great listener. The phone rang while they were chatting away and enjoying their visit. "Jessie" the neighbour called to her daughter, "see who is calling the Jewett's". This lady had no shame at being known as an eavesdropper. But as we had all known it anyway, it was no big deal.

The listening in was seldom malicious. With our lack of social life, this was one way of keeping in touch. If this lady heard a call for help, she would be the first to offer her services. There was no listening in on our phone. My mother was a real lady, and she believed this was a violation of privacy. There were many others who also had the same opinion as my mother. The one time that Mother let her hair down was when there was sickness in a home. She would take down the receiver and listen until she heard how the ill family was faring and quietly hang up.

We were a considerable distance from a doctor, and "ambulance" was a word that we had probably never heard. When help was needed, one long ring GENERAL ALARM was cranked out. It sent messages to all. Everyone was expected to listen to this one. It was great for a burning building, an accident, or any of the other things that could and did go wrong at times. In just no time at all, help was on the way. It surely was much faster than our present mail service!

Many a romance was aided by the telephone. People lived a few miles apart and cars were very scarce. Each couple devised their own code to fool the eavesdroppers. One couple came up with what they thought was a fool proof idea. They set a time in the evening when they thought no one would be using the phone. They were all farmers in the community and went to bed early. At a given time, each one went to their respective phone and lifted the receiver. There was no ring, therefore they had privacy. This worked brilliantly for a time and they were very smug in thinking they had outsmarted the nosy ones. One evening, our most famous "listening queen" decided to make a late call before she went to bed. Imagine her surprise when she interrupted some very hot love talk!

Mrs. Listening Queen felt very thwarted when she realized that someone had pulled the wool over her eyes, or in this case over her ears. Her pride was hurt that they had the nerve to converse behind her back! It didn't take her very long to realize how it was done. That was the last time the love birds had any privacy. The "listening queen" was still the reigning monarch!

Some years ago I went into a museum, and there was the exact replica of our old wall phones. When growing up it was part of our every day lives, and was taken for granted. Now I realize how important it really was. It saved lives, brought good news or bad, and help when most needed. In fact I think it was one of the most important items in our daily lives. Most of all, there was also the knowledge that there was always someone there on the other end when needed.

WEATHER

The weather was extremely cold in winter but could be very hot in summer. I remember one summer in the second year on the farm after we had been married, we had frost in every month of the year. Thank heavens that wasn't always the case.

Our homes were always heated by wood. There was the box stove or heater in the living room and the cooking stove in the kitchen. In the summer the house was so hot that the heat was unbearable. Most people had summer kitchens. This was a lean-to added on the side of the house and opening off the kitchen. In the spring everything was moved out to the summer kitchen and all the cooking was done there. It kept the other areas of the house much cooler. As soon as fall came the kitchen was moved back in. The cook fires were very welcome then. We never had a summer kitchen, our house and everything in it was burned before I was born. There were five children then. It was a hard time for my parents to get another house built from scratch, along with more children coming. Dad never seemed to get that summer kitchen built. There was a lot of sickness, and other things that took whatever could be scraped up. We had a very small house. I will never know how Mother managed in just three rooms until I was thirteen or fourteen. There were eight kids, but never that many at once. My brother Larry was working out before I, the seventh, was born. My next two sisters, Hazel and Lena, were out working when my brother Jim was born. There was always company at our house. Travelling was slow and relatives came and stayed for a day or two. They also had large families. It was nothing new for us to be lying in rows on the floor like overgrown stuffed sausages when we had company. The boys many times bedded down on blankets in the barn on the hay in the summer time.

Mother always made us bring in four pails of water and an enormous supply of wood before going to bed. In the morning, the water would have a good depth of ice on it. The tea kettle on the stove would have ice in it also. Not having any storm windows, there was always a thick frost covering the panes. The frost was great for scribbling your initials.

Many times during the night when we were having an extreme cold snap, we would be awakened by what sounded like rifle shots. It would be the trees snapping in the frost. The nails pulling free in the house made themselves heard quite frequently.

A full moon seemed to be full brother to frost and cold. I can never remember one without the other. Looking out the window was to behold one of the most beautiful sights: the moon shining on the white snow and everything glistening; the trees wearing a heavy coating of frost, and making shadows on the snow that looked like magic. The coyotes did their serenading during the full moon. As kids we were terrified of them. It was weird and frightening, but since I have become an adult it is like chamber music to me.

We saw the northern lights many times during the winter. It was always so beautiful that we awakened everybody to see them. At their most majestic, they were coloured. I can't remember seeing the coloured ones on too many occasions, but they were really something to see, all reds, pinks, greens, blues, and changing all the time. They were never the same for a second.

In the winter all horses had bells. No sleigh or cutter that I have ever seen had head lamps, so this was one way of letting the other travellers know that you were there. Each person had his own individual taste in bells. People with driving horses (not working draft horses) would have a whole band of one, two or three inch bells. Work horses would usually have two larger bells that hung on the hames. They all sounded different. If you were walking down the road and heard horse bells, they were usually identified by the sound. They really were individual and different. The one thing about them was that they sounded so great. To be out on a cold frosty night on a sleigh or cutter and hearing the bells on the frosty air is something that will never be recaptured. It is one of my nicest memories.

Because our house was small, Mother made us play out as much as possible. We used to sleigh ride and ski. Of course as we got older, we had to work. Our parents gave us a reasonable amount of work to do. When it was finished, we could play. But if the work was not finished, no playing. We always made sure it was done. There is something to be said for large families and working together. It wasn't too hard to work when everyone else was working along beside you. Many times it was a joint effort and the work seemed like fun.

March brought many storms. It was also the beginning of tree tapping for the maple syrup season. The best sap weather was frosty nights and sunny days. The sun melted the snow just enough to make a beautiful crust overnight. This was melted again by noon next day. The children were put outside to play all morning and could run around on the crust with no trouble. It was unexcelled for sleigh or toboggan riding.

It could also be a time for flooding. Between our home and the highway was a field about half a mile square. It had two creeks running through it, both crossing our side road. The whole field was a lake, which was both a blessing and a nuisance. When it froze over, it was a gorgeous skating rink, but when it was open it was a horse of a different colour. We, who could ski, could glide across most of it or avoid the current, but there was no easy way. When my brother Jim was born on the 8th of March, it took some head scratching to come up with a way in for the midwife.

We had a lane down to our side road, and then as it went on past our place, it was a straight half-mile to the highway. We were the last family on the side road. There was one other family on it, but they had an optional way out.

Every winter most men, ours included, worked in the lumber camps with the team of horses. The only way we had of getting around was walking, skiing or snowshoes. The zigzag rail fences on each side were level with the snow. It was a real snow tunnel. We used to complain about having to walk through this to school, but were reminded by my mother that when she used the road, there were more traces of use over against the fence than there were down the middle. We assured her we only used the fences to jump into the snowdrifts. By the second or third storm the snow was level and there was no place to jump.

There was soon a path that was pretty well packed by children, dogs, sleighs and skis. Most years when Dad returned home from the camps in late March or early April, it would be about nine or ten o'clock at night. But how did they get the horses through that hard packed snow? The path was not very wide and would not accommodate both horses; and off to the side of the path, the snow was almost as high as their backs. But good old Bob and Roy were ready for anything and glad to be home. Dad solved the problem by hitching one behind the other and then to the sleigh.

One year, on the first day of May, the road still level to the fences with snow, my dad and my two brothers started to shovel the road out. By the second day, Mother Nature came along and helped out with a warming rain.

Our pump used to freeze during the night and then we had to pour hot water down it to thaw the cylinder. That was one reason Mom made sure we had the water pails filled at night.

Summer was lovely. We went barefoot, both by necessity and choice. Each night, after the weather started to warm, we tested to see if we might go barefoot tomorrow. And how great it felt to squeeze the dust between our toes. We always had to put on shoes if we went to the fields as the hay and grain stubble could skin your toes if they weren't protected. At supper time there was always a tub of water left out for warming up. When we were ready for bed, we all washed our feet in the nicely warmed water.

Summertime meant berry picking and harvesting. It also meant new stock, calves, lambs and pigs. The men had been cutting wood all winter long whenever they had time. After being sawed in stove lengths, the pieces were split and piled. We had to pile and stack wood every night for a certain length of time. The wood for the cook stove was split very fine and was piled as near as possible to the house before we had a wood shed. The wood for the box stove could be left a little larger. It was piled near at hand also. There was always a large amount of wood ready to be sold, if we were lucky enough to have a buyer. This could be stacked away from the house. This wood wasn't split but we had to be careful when piling it; if it was piled right, it was easily measured.

Because wood was so plentiful, we had to spend an exceedingly large number of hours at that job. We started in early spring. As soon as we arrived home from school, we changed our clothes and stacked wood for an hour. After supper we did the chores and then went out and stacked for another hour.

This went on until late June. There was one exciting reason to finish this up when we got near the last of it. There was always a deep layer of ice and snow under it. When the last stick of wood was piled we had ice cream. This was the homemade type with real cream and eggs that weren't even a day old. Mom made a plentiful supply for us. We didn't in the beginning have a freezer. We gathered a large dishpan of ice and salt. In this we had a large covered mixing bowl with the custard in it. This was probably the only time all year we would see ice cream. I thought I would never again taste anything so great.

The daylight seemed to last until quite late. This is where I learned to love softball. The whip-poor-wills were our time clock. When they sounded their nightly serenades, it was time to go home. At ten minutes to nine, you could bet your bottom dollar the whip-poor-will would sing. There was no daylight saving time yet and wherever we would be playing, we hastened home at the first call. I doubt if the whip-poor-will ever heeded the daylight saving time so I expect he is calling at ten to ten. Just a case of the whole world being out of step!

I mentioned earlier our very small house. My mother had been working on Dad for years to do something about it, but it isn't easy when there is no money. It was just at the beginning of the depression that changes had to be made. At home there were my parents, three brothers, and another sister beside myself. My oldest brother had just been laid off his job, and there was no other job to go to. Sometimes there was a part time one, but it was not always possible to collect your wages. There were line ups everywhere of men seeking work. We invited his wife and their two children to stay with us. Not even Mother could manage ten people in a three-room house. But where there is a will, there is a way. There used to be a small village about five or six miles west of us. Many people had moved away. Dad inquired about one of the abandoned cottages. He found he could buy one for $15.00; yes, a bargain, but still a lot of money. We scratched up a few dollars here and there, sold a little more wood and bought it. This was in the fall and every spare hour that could be found was spent in dismantling that cottage. Everything had to be done so carefully and saved. The nails were thrown into a box and brought home each night. It was my job to straighten and sort them into sizes. I never in all my life had such sore fingers. I pounded them, but got more dextrous as the weeks went by. The three men took their lunches and the team of horses each day and went to Kenabutch to work. They brought home a load each night. At noon they boiled a billy of tea, and thawed themselves and their sandwiches out by toasting them over a fire.

When the frost was out, the building began. The east side of the house, we decided, was the proper place for the addition. We built a kitchen, bedroom, pantry and storage room. It was great, but in other peoples' eyes still no large house.

There was one special corner that we called the chimney corner. There was a space of about 24 inches from the chimney to the wall. We had a shelf built there. It was the perfect place to let the bread rise, thaw things out, or just to slip there to warm yourself. It was a favourite place for mittens or socks to dry.

One year Mom wanted a sink. We had no running water inside, but even not having to carry it out would be a help. We had heard of a load of pipe that was for sale in Massey. We knew we would need washers, elbows, joints etc. besides the standard piping. Well, nothing ventured, nothing gained. When we inquired about it, the man in charge said, "If you will take the whole damned thing off my hands you can have the works for a dollar. WOW!" So we had our sink and were the envy of all the other housewives around.

We were also the first family to have an ice house. By this time the members of the family who were working out put ideas in our head. Dad had already made us a little wash house from leftover items from the house addition. Now he built the icehouse. One of my sisters bought a second hand ice box for us and we thought we were in seventh heaven. It is very hard to keep food when there is no cold place; this made a super change for the better in keeping perishables.

NEIGHBOURHOOD CHARACTER #1

Walking down the street, a short time ago, my eyes lighted on a gentleman leaving his car. The car had stalled and to say he was angry was a gross understatement! He gave the tires a couple of kicks and let forth some explosive language that would have put a stevedore to shame. It took me back to my early married days, and a character who thought his car was a living object and a most cherished possession. He talked to and petted that old car; that is when it was doing its job! When it failed to obey him, he took it personally. Then there were fireworks. It was more like a husband and wife battling except that poor old Lizzie didn't talk back. Perhaps that is why Benny loved his car so much. He always had the last word!

The car was a very ancient Model T. I am sure it must have been 1918 or 1920 era. It had lost its top many years before I knew it. It had to be cranked; that alone was sometimes an entertainment in itself, to hear the colourful language used by Benny when it didn't fire the first time or two, for Benny had a terrific temper!

There were two levers on the steering wheel. I think they were the gas and spark. Was that gas lever the first cruise control? The brake was a lever on the floor. It was amazing what he could get from that ancient scrap heap when it was in the mood. It was war time and no spare parts were available; I doubt if they were available for that particular Model, even if parts were not restricted.

Benny must have been a genius in his own right to even keep it going at all. It is mind boggling what a bit of haywire, binder twine, pieces of wood, and nails will do!

He had a love-hate going on with that car at all times. When it performed well he called it love names, praised it, and could never go by without giving it a loving pat or two.

He lived on a back road by a lake and had a two-room shack that was a perfect match for his vehicle. There was no telephone or any modern conveniences in his home. He scratched out a small garden and had an old shed where he worked on his car. Benny never married, but never lacked for companionship, because he had his Lizzie. He could carry on a conversation with her for hours. She never answered him back, or railed at him for being unemployed; nor did she want money for clothing and non-essentials. His only gripe with his beloved Lizzie was that at times she became unmanageable, and refused to run. When this happened, it was a sight to behold!

Benny had no full time job. He just worked around for the farmers when the mood suited him, or when he needed some ready cash. When he had a few bucks in his jeans he quit. Benny was a good worker, and if you could hire him for a few days you could consider yourself fortunate for he did an excellent job. We were always happy to have him. Farm workers were not rationed but were very scarce. The good meals he received were a bonus to him. He mostly looked like a walking scarecrow and was not known for his culinary expertise at home. You might say that the appearance of his car, clothing, and living quarters were a matching threesome.

One summer he had agreed to help us with the haying for a week or so. We needed a part for the mower that day, so Benny offered to drive to town and pick it up. He invited me to go, as well, to pick up groceries and catch up on business affairs while there. The rad had a slow leak and on the way home, Benny remembered he had not filled it up in town. He pulled the car to the side of the road by a water-filled ditch. As he was about to apply the brakes, he jammed his foot down; he was wearing loose-legged jeans and the gear lever went up his pant leg. Any normal person would have just lifted his leg and removed it; but not Benny! He just shook and kept on shaking that leg back and forth with the most hair raising threats and curses I had ever heard. I hastily covered my year old son's ears in case some of this was impressed on him. I tried my best to keep my amusement to myself until later when I shared it with my husband. Everyone had a Benny story to tell, and they usually were repeated at some time or other so that he became known as a neighbourhood character.

One day, when he was about a mile from home, about three quarters of the way up a very steep hill, the car refused to go any further. There were two other neighbours with him. They got out and threw a fence rail behind the wheels so that it couldn't change its mind and back down the hill. Benny did all that he could and thought that poor Lizzie might at least co-operate. This was one of the hate times. The other two men tried everything they knew but the car positively refused to move; after all it was dying of old age and was in its last throes of life. Finally he started to punch it with his fists. When his fists were too sore and this car still refused to start, Benny was in quite a temper. He reached into the back seat and found an axe. He caved in that poor old car wherever he could. At the same time he was pouring out all of his frustrations with his once dearly loved Lizzie. He remembered all the times she had let him down in the years they had spent together. He never missed a shortcoming or a weakness. He then asked the two neighbours who were with him to help push it over the ditch to some rocks. After trying to change his mind, they finally helped him to push it away. There he gave it an extra shove and sent it flying over the edge to tumble down to the bottom. As the poor old car thumped and bumped to a shuddering stop, Benny stood there frustrated, sad, angry, and sorry, tears streaming down his face. The only love he had ever had was no more!

NEIGHBOURHOOD CHARACTER #2

One of our most memorable neighbours was named Albert. I don't know much of his history before I came as a newly married wife to our farm. My husband had known Albert all of his life, but there was always so much in the present about him to keep us amused that we forgot about the past. I regret never asking what he was like in his earlier years.

Albert was such a dirty Raggedy Andy person, I can only judge his age as about sixty when I first saw him, but through the years that I knew him, he seemed always the same. He just never aged; of course it was a bit hard to tell. His long untrimmed hair and whiskers, his tattered dirty clothing and his entire dishevelment threw you off and his age never entered your mind. Winter or summer, he was always clad in several layers of shirts or vest and always a coat with large pockets. It was amazing what went into those large pockets.

Some years before I knew him, he met a widow with many daughters. Ada had lost her husband some time before, and she had been doing her very best to keep the home together and the family fed. She must have been really desperate. In the early thirties there were just no jobs available for either men or women. There were no suitors asking for her hand. Well, almost none! There was Albert, who loved his food and comforts and had no one to cook for him; now here was Ada who was noted for her fine cooking, cleanliness, and was a great worker to boot. He seemed to think they would make a great match.

Albert had a much neglected farm and a few animals. Work and Albert were not on friendly terms. Had he taken into consideration that he would be responsible for eight or ten people? He finally popped the question and Ada said "yes". Or did Ada do the asking? I just don't know.

Perhaps she thought with their combined efforts they might manage. But poor Albert just didn't make it. After a few years Ada decided to leave. By this time several of the girls had left home, and some had married.

I never knew Albert until he was back to being a single (eligible?) male again. If ever Ada had cleaned him up, I would love to have seen it. One time, when I heard him being questioned about her leaving, he was asked what he thought of that. Albert replied, "Well, when I came in and sat down on the last chair, they pulled it right out from under me backside and left". (Not his exact words!)

Quite frequently when one answered a knock on the door, there was Albert in all his tatters. "I say, ma'am, would you like to make me a couple of pies?" This was a frequent request. He always said he would pay for them. His idea of payment was about a quarter of what was bakery price, or better still, no payment at all. He was a great moocher. His next request would be for homemade bread. Most of us made our own bread and he never quit pestering us for it. He stated that because he ate more homemade bread, a loaf didn't last as long as it should, so it should be worth less. He never missed a housewife in the area – that is, the good bakers! He certainly never bothered the lousy cooks. Once, upon receiving a couple of pies from me that I had baked for him, he left very happily with the pies tipped sideways under his arm and the juice running down his coat.

One of my nightmares was of Albert taking my young son on his knee and wanting to feed him from his plate. I did try to keep Warren away from him, but he was always a curious boy and for some reason was fascinated with Albert; probably because he had never seen anyone just like him. Warren just wanted to be around when Albert was there. Albert always knew what time to visit to be invited to a meal. One evening I had cooked half of a large cauliflower from our garden. He had never seen one before and I had to explain to him what it was. He said he liked it and of course I believed him because after he had gone I found he had slipped the other half into one of his voluminous pockets.

One day in early spring, after many days of rain, my husband was passing Albert's place when he was invited in. Jim had a pretty iron stomach when it came to food and was mostly ready to try anything, but there was just no way that he would stay for a meal there. Albert had just brought a pail of water from the spring and was going to make tea. He took a look at it and saw that it was slightly brown from the run off of the barn yard. "I say, it won't take too many tea bags to make a pot of tea in that." My husband left like a shot. No way was he going to have a cup of tea or anything else there. Jim said he didn't know if Albert was fooling or not, but he didn't dare take the chance. He said: "You know Vern, when I went in I thought I might close my eyes, and my mind, and have a cup of tea; after all what could he do to a cup of tea? You can be sure I will never go near that place again."

One year we had a twister that had blown through and left quite a lot of damage. The neighbours all banded together and helped until the damage was repaired. When it was Albert's turn to have his barn repaired, the ladies sent plenty of food and baking; none of the men were quite prepared to eat his baking. The men kidded him and reminded him that some beer might go well as it was hot sunny weather. He faithfully promised them that he would provide the beer.

When the morning came and the men set to work, Albert, true to his word, produced the beer. All at once there was a roar from the men with the most terrific swearing and confusion going on. Albert had gone to the spring and brought back a two gallon pail of nice cold water. He then emptied a pint bottle of beer into the bucket. He tried to explain to the disconcerted men that there was no reason to get excited as he also had another bottle for the afternoon!

During the time that Albert was married, his wife had a hopeless job trying to make him keep enough wood for the household. She was a great cook and couldn't bake those delicacies without wood for her oven.

One year, my husband was clearing up a corner field by the road past our farm. He was throwing the limbs and unusable trash on the stumps to try to burn them.

The Balm of Gilead trees were always a headache to kill. Anyone who has ever tried to burn it, will know what I mean. Trying to get some heat from it was like trying to burn cement or chalk. The wood never dried up enough to burn. You couldn't kill the roots of the tree. You might think you had them gone when, the next year, they sprouted up thirty or forty feet away.

One day Albert came driving along in his buggy. He saw Jim at work; his bright eyes saw this beautiful wood going to waste. "I say, Jimmie, could you spare me some of that wood? I am just about out of wood, and Ada is just about out of patience." Jim was not a bit put out about having the nuisance wood taken off his hands. Albert loaded some into the buggy and was back in the evening for a wagon load.

Albert had a couple of days work on a road job. The day after presenting Ada with all the wood she would need for a while, he thought he was home free. At noon time, hungry and anticipating a good substantial lunch, he opened his lunch box and opened up the wax paper. He let out a bellow that could be heard in the next county. He disgustedly threw down his lunch for all to see. It consisted of one generous slice of raw meat enclosed in two slices of raw bread dough.

NEIGHBOURHOOD CHARACTER #3

Men were not the only characters where I grew up. Some of the women could be just as kooky as any man I ever knew.

The first one that comes to mind is Mrs. B. Everyone knew her or knew of her. She was famous in her own way. If she was not known to you personally, someone just had to mention her name and someone would start on the stories that circulated. Mrs. B. created more good belly laughs than anyone I ever knew.

Mrs. B's housekeeping left something to be desired. In fact, it could be compared fairly with Albert's, our second character whom I wrote of earlier. Her hair was scraggly, and, to be kind, had a shampoo about every six months. Her clothes were always filthy, with unmended rips and tears here and there. One wonders if her clothes were ever washed, or even her body. She often wore her husband's boots, well covered with barn manure. I suppose she liked them well seasoned! Her apron was an old potato sack that had never been washed since it had been used for the potatoes.

My first visit to her home was with my sister-in-law who lived close by. This was to be just a short stop and it was just that. Mrs. B. could be very friendly when she wanted. She could also become belligerent and fractious when the occasion arose. This was one of her friendly times. She was going to make a pot of tea for us that we promptly refused as we had more urgent things that would take us away very shortly. First of all we had to clear a chair before we could be seated. The stench in the house was unbelievable. There were a couple of dogs and a cat. The chickens also came freely through the open door. There were bits of harness, potato sacks, pieces of rope and many other items from farm living which were usually kept in the out buildings.

There were no screen doors. One hen came in and flew on to the table to gather up the crumbs and a crust of bread. When she had finished her snack, she promptly dipped her tail and left her calling card. Mrs. B. just picked it off in her hand and threw it out the door. She then took the dish cloth and wiped up the table! When Mabel and I left, I was actually sick. Mabel was not quite as affected as I, as she had grown up with them and had gone to school with the girls. She didn't like it, but she was seldom surprised as I had been.

When our church group put on a chicken dinner, it was an event. Chickens were hard to come by even if we were on a farm. In those days this was pricey food. Mrs. B. lived four miles away in the next village. She was a podgy short lady who could almost eat a tenth of her own weight at a sitting. That was if it was someone else's food! We were astounded at the amounts she could manage. Then one evening, she was piling on her plate, more than any of us had seen her do before. We had one not quite sober young man who insisted on helping us. "Mrs. B." he said, "Eat all you want but please don't put any in your pocket." To our consternation, she was doing just that! Pieces of chicken, a couple of rolls, cookies and whatever else that wasn't liquid. We had no doubt what the condition of her clothes was; but then of course they weren't that great to start with. We had to stop her of course, but not before she gave us a good piece of her mind. She was well watched after that whenever she appeared at any of our other social activities.

These were depression days and a social evening was usually a dance in someone's home. The ladies brought the lunch. The music was supplied by anyone who had an instrument and some talent. Some of my nicest memories are of these most informal evenings.

My sister-in-law's family was very musical and had open house many times. Mabel used to laugh and tell us how they delegated one of the children to watch and see what Mrs. B., or her family, contributed. This contribution was then set aside and accidentally misplaced, or dropped, and eventually ended up on the pigs' diet the next day. Mrs. B. sometimes offered her home for one of these functions. She probably had her mind set on the leftovers. When the dance was to be held there, Mabel, her sisters and a few of their friends went over and gave the place a real cleaning and did what they could. It was a home, where, if you spilled something, or made a mess, there was nothing damaged.

Spanish, the section where they lived, had no electricity or bathrooms. At these dances the girls wouldn't go outside to the outhouse, as there were always men standing round. Upstairs there were chamber pots or "thunder mugs" as we used to call them. A couple of the boys who prided themselves on being jokesters, decided to have a wee bit of fun! They went upstairs in Mrs. B's house and slipped into the bedroom the girls would be using. There they dropped Seidlitz powders into one of the "mugs" where they were completely invisible against the white china of the "mug". If you are old enough, you will remember this was a white powder that came in two packs. This was used for headaches and sick stomachs. Each pack could be dropped in liquid and nothing happened. But when combined they fizzed and climbed the sides of the glass in frenzy to reach up and over.

Now the lads who supplied the powders did nothing by halves. They put several packages into the "mug". After all they had to ensure that their powder was not wasted. When the party was well under way, several of the girls went upstairs to do what they had to do. There were several "mugs" ready for use, so a couple of the girls used one, then a German girl used the other. When the Seidlitz powders began their job, she jumped up screaming: "Mien Gott, Mien Gott, I am fissing." In the excitement, they upset one of the chamber pots, where it ran through the floor; as there was no ceiling down below, the contents landed on a cake pan, complete with cake. Mrs. B. was there and she didn't get too perturbed at the accident. She poured off the liquid and was heard to explain that it was still edible. Of course this made quite a to do in the kitchen, and she fought quite valiantly to save the cake, but the kitchen gang said: "NO WAY" and it was sent to the pigs right then. Mrs. B. wasn't above using it the next day if it had been left!

MISHAPS

Dreamily doing the dishes one morning, I was intensely aware of the beautiful March weather. The sun was making sparkling diamonds from last night's frost. I was thinking what a shame that although the sun was making such a beautiful display, it would last for only a short time before the sparkles melted away. Suddenly I saw my husband actually flying about six feet up in the air. Shocked, I ran as fast as my legs could carry me. Our dog was barking and creating quite a fuss. He had cornered a cow and was holding her by the barn. My eyes went to Jim to find him getting to his feet. Most unbelievably, he was unhurt. The cow in question had had a new calf the day before. When the cows were let out of the stable for the day, the new mother saw Jim and his shadow, our dog Blackie, starting for the stable. She knew her calf was inside and felt it was threatened, so made a charge at him. She had short horns and just tossed him into the air like a light weight. We finally got things set to rights and examined the damage. He was wearing a very tough pair of Army surplus trousers, which had a six inch three cornered tear. His underwear had a two inch tear, and his skin was barely grazed. There was no other damage. It just was his lucky day.

Jim worked long days on the farm and was a perfectionist about most things. But he was accident prone.

When my family left the farm we took over their collie dog. From the first he rarely left my husband's side. When Jim went up the ladder to the hayloft, Blackie followed. When Jim came back down the ladder, Blackie decided he did much better on the up grade than on the down. He whined until Jim went up and had to carry him down. When they were half way down, Blackie got quite excited and started to scramble around. It threw Jim off balance and they both fell the rest of the way. There were some bad bruises but not serious ones. He had a time trying to discourage Blackie from following him up the ladder. Once in a while he tried it again, but never managed to come down the ladder by himself.

We had a circular saw and one day Jim was going to cut up some surplus wood that he had around. He was having a bit of trouble as he had flooded the engine. It stopped a couple of times and I heard a few cuss words. I was hanging out my washing at the time. Finally the motor started, then stalled. There was dead silence. It alarmed me as I fully expected to hear another cuss or two. I ran around the corner and found him lying on the ground in a dazed way. The blood was pouring from his chin and temple. With my excellent first aid training, I finally got the bleeding stopped. I backed the car around to where he was lying and struggled with his six foot body. He was still in a semi conscious state and not much help. I brought a pillow and a blanket and settled him in the back seat. I was vastly relieved when we arrived at the doctor's office. He had multiple stitches and was in shock. The scar on his chin was like a dimple for the rest of his life.

It was evening before he could tell me what had happened. He had tried the saw with a piece of wood. The wood had a bit of branch on it that he hadn't noticed.

Jamming, it caught and pulled him into the saw. That was the last he remembered. He had very vague memories of the trip to the doctor.

Then there was the summer that was probably the very worst of my life, certainly it was the most memorable! We had finished haying and Jim had gone to help a neighbour. I was beginning to get worried as he was so late getting home. When he finally arrived, it was with a neighbour bringing him home with a cast on his leg. He had been thrown off a truckload of hay and landed on hard ground.

I was very sick at the time, but there was just no way that I could dodge my responsibilities. Finding a spare man in the area was a pipe dream as it was still war time.

I had hepatitis and was unable to eat. I also had a super active two-year-old son. I had to do the milking and care for the stock, not to mention all of the other chores around the place. Jim did what he could but the doctor had told him to keep off the leg. Then ten days later I broke out with shingles. We got a man for a day when we could, but this kind of help was very rare. My usual weight then was 120; I ended up at 90 pounds that summer.

One winter, just after Christmas, Jim brought in an arm full of wood. As he deposited it, his foot slipped on some snow on the linoleum and he fell across the wood box breaking two ribs on his left side. He had his side taped up for six weeks. One Saturday he went into town and had the doctor remove the tape. He came home declaring himself a new man to have that aggravating tape off his ribs. Next day, Sunday, he was walking past a pile of logs and decided one stood out a few inches. Well, I did say he was a perfectionist about some things, and also that he was accident prone. He reached over to straighten that log. It knocked several others out of place and yes, you got it – he broke two ribs on his right side. So he struggled through another six weeks of healing his ribs and saying favourite cuss words about the tape and the pain.

Jim & Verna home for Christmas in 1942.

When he went out to the doctor and had his tape removed again, he thought he was home free. No so! That same evening he was feeding the stock when one cow, waiting eagerly for her turn, swung her head around and caught him on the left side and broke two ribs there!

He had spent the whole winter nursing broken ribs. I think we might call it "The Winter of Mishaps".

BEST FRIENDS

Tap, tap, tap! As I went to the door to answer that little timid summons, I knew it would be May. She had her own special signal and I always looked forward to seeing her. Yes, it was May and she had, as usual, a little gift for us.

May and her husband Bill were the poorest people, money wise, that I ever knew. Whenever we visited her or if she visited us, there was always some little gift or offering. Today, it was a roast of venison and some liver. Liver is not the love of my life, but Jim loved it. She had shot the deer herself. It had been eating the tender young grain that was just showing above the ground. She dressed it up herself and had canned most of it in jars.

May's husband, Bill, was just about the laziest man that you might find. He was not bad looking, liked to indulge in a bit of bragging, but was very good natured and easy going. He could do a good day's work if he was at a neighbour's, but at home left everything for his wife to do. May absolutely adored him; she thought of him as something from Heaven sent just for her. Now of course, he never abused her, didn't drink, and never looked at another woman, so he did have some things going for him.

They lived on a poor run down farm just south of us. It was over two miles by road and one half mile through the bush. We were great friends and used that path through the woods quite often. She didn't have many other close friends. Of course there was a scarcity of women in that area.

May was born to a couple who just sort of took her for granted and she became the work horse for the family. She had no more than three or four years of schooling. She was always needed more at home. When a younger brother appeared upon the scene, he became a sort of God to the family. He was made to be waited on, and May became the waiter. Girls were so useless in this world. (Sic Sic!) So it is no wonder that she saw nothing wrong in waiting on her husband so faithfully.

May and her husband lived in a one room log cabin. They had a small barn, also built of logs, and there were a few other buildings. There were only about 20 or 30 tillable acres and no one ever could hope to make a living from them. But somehow she managed. She cut wood and sold it in town, loading it and delivering it to her customers. Now she was only about five feet tall but she was a mighty lady. Her muscles would put Mike Tyson's to shame.

One evening we had walked down to their place and she told us she was just about to move the hay rack onto the wagon. Jim remarked that it was good timing for her as he would do it for her. But of course she insisted on helping him. He took one end and she took the other end. He remarked on the way home, that even though it was heavy, she didn't seem to notice. Jim was a very strong man, and he thought it was heavy. She would take the team and hay rack out to the fields and load it, then unload at the barn. Sometimes she had a bit of help from Bill, but not too often. There was always something more urgent for him to do a few miles away.

She had five or six sheep which she sheared herself. She also had a spinning wheel and made up her own wool on it. She would dye some of it and sell quite a few skeins. She had a few things like this that brought her in a bit of hard-to-come-by cash. When she found out that my husband could chew the heels from his socks almost as fast as I could knit them, she made some especially thick to take care of that and of course it worked.

One time, Bill came in to visit us and was very, very excited. He said that May was "pregmated" and they were most excited. Somehow they must have read the signs wrong, for the baby never materialized. They were very disappointed. When she knew that we were expecting, she couldn't have been kinder. She made custards and soup to help soothe my upset stomach. She would knit many pairs of tiny mitts or socks for my son over the years. When four years later, I was expecting my daughter, she did the same things.

She had some hens and a few geese. One spring she brought up a couple of very cherished goose eggs for Warren to hatch out with the help of a brooding hen.

When she knew that we were having threshers or woodcutters with a big crew of men to feed, she would be right there to help. And she was a great help. She would have been up at an early hour to milk and feed her own animals before appearing at our place.

They grew such a wee bit of grain that she threshed some of it herself and fed some to the stock as is. She had a large vegetable garden and grew some potatoes and turnips for sale. She grew an abundance of beans, which were dried and shelled. She would often bring me a large pot of these beans when she came. In berry season, she picked blueberries and sold some, as well as canned them. In the fall she picked cranberries. If you didn't mind wading in icy cold water, they were easily picked. She found a great market for these at Christmas.

When she came up through the woods to visit us, she would usually have a .22 with her for rabbits or partridge. If she had any luck on the way up, she wanted to share with us. She was a crack shot and didn't have too many misses. Jim used to say she could shoot the eye out of a squirrel at a half mile.

When I broke the news to her that we would be moving to Southern Ontario, she was very disappointed and told me how she would miss us. Well, we knew we would miss her too and were exceedingly sad. Our children were very fond of her also.

When it came time to pack, she was right there to help me. The last day she came, she had, as usual, a gift. She had no money to spend on a gift so she made one. She had taken a quantity of white feathers and dyed them pink. She then sewed them on white cotton (flour bag). It was a lovely gift and I treasured it for years. I could only imagine the work she put into that cushion with hand picking the feathers, dying them, etc. It was difficult to say goodbye to a friend like that. We were both in an advanced state of tears when we parted. Neither of us has ever had such a friend before or since.

HIDDEN DANGERS

Reflecting back on our memoirs we tend to remember the good things and forget the unpleasant ones. This was brought to my attention recently while on a long distance call from my nephew.

Marvin, from 11 to 13 thirteen years of age, had stayed with us on the farm for his summer vacations. He reminded me of a couple of very dangerous episodes that had occurred while staying with us. I had completely forgotten them until reminded; but the memories certainly came back then. It sometimes takes only a nudge to recover them. That night we were on the phone for an hour.

On one occasion, I had taken Marvin, then twelve, and my two-year-old son, Warren, for a visit with May. My friend, May, lived more than half a mile to the south of us through the woods. It was several miles by road, so we always used the old bush road and walked there.

After a short but pleasant visit with May, we left to come home. I carried Warren who was a wiggly, but light, burden.

In the summer, our cows always roamed the bush and found plenty of grazing. As we were almost at the fence into the field by home, Marvin let out a shriek that would have frightened Dracula. "The bull, the bull!" he cried. Our huge bull was always fenced in his own separate field, but this afternoon had decided to find himself greener pastures. He demolished the fence and was now among the cows. He roared (louder than Marvin had) and came at a gallop after us. Our race to the fence and safety would have shamed the Olympic contenders; and that bull, for all his size, could really move. We made it to the fence with just a margin to spare. I actually threw Warren over the fence and was over it myself almost as he hit the ground. Marvin was right there with us, and we were on our feet and on our way within a split second. From there, it was only a very short sprint to the house and safety, where we all recuperated from our shattered nerves.

One evening in July, I went out to pick wild strawberries. It was after the evening chores were done. Jim was working in the yard and would look after Warren.

The weather was abnormally cold, so I went out wearing a heavy dark jacket and slacks. The berries were plentiful and I had a fair sized pail full for pies next day; but it was almost dark, as I made my way home. Just back of the barn, I climbed the last fence and in minutes I was home.

About five minutes later there was a knock at the door; it was Albert, a neighbour from the next farm who had been out hunting for a deer. As he was drinking his coffee, he commented that he had just missed out on a bear. He had the rifle, he explained, and was aiming it at a bear as it was going over the fence, but it disappeared so fast, he couldn't shoot. He rarely, if ever, missed when he fired. The three of us were in deep shock when we realized I was the bear! It was also my son's first birthday. How nearly he came to growing up without his mother.

Another year that Marvin spent with us was even more nerve wracking, but not a race for our lives like the other one.

My in-laws lived a mile away. The first half mile had bush lots on either side of the road; then open fields and farms to their house.

Marvin and I had visited with Grandma and Grandpa Thaxter. It was dark when we left for home. At that time it was quite safe to walk home in the dark. There was seldom anyone else on the road.

We walked past the open fields, and were half way through the wooded part of the path when I had a very uncanny feeling as if we were being followed. I tried to shake it off, but it persisted. I was not too disturbed by this at first, but after a few minutes I was very frightened. I talked quietly to Marvin and told him that we would have to walk a little faster. "Just keep walking naturally," I told him, "but a little faster."

I had to keep reassuring him to keep my own fears at bay. We kept on talking and were soon in sight of the house.

We were discussing this with Jim. He thought that we might have imagined it as something like this had never happened before.

A few minutes later there was a real cacophony of wolves howling at the edge of the field by our house. They had followed us home! Jim, the next day, apologized for doubting us.

Jim's brother, Ron, was a woodsman, and in later years had become a professional trapper. After the episode of the wolves, he went after them and killed one. That must have discouraged the others for they never came back. They were probably after the sheep when they decided to follow us.

LICENCE TO DRIVE

When I began keeping company with Jim, he had an old 29 Chev. At home, we never had a car, so I looked forward to driving. Jim had been away, off and on, the first summer, and then we had both been in the city, so the car had been up on blocks at home. I never did get the opportunity to learn.

We lived in the city a few years until Jim got the urge to get back to the farm. He really liked farming, and we had one just waiting for us.

We were given a horse for a wedding present, but we needed another. Gas was rationed and we decided to sell the old Chev to buy a horse to complete the team. We were six miles from town but Jim's dad had a car and lived only a mile away. We made out nicely with his help.

A few years later, we had decided to buy a farm in Southern Ontario. We knew we would be needing a car, so now we purchased a '31 Ford. Here was my opportunity to learn to drive. To my delight and amazement, my husband was the first one to mention that it was time I had some driving lessons.

But my father-in-law was not quite as eager for me to learn as Jim was. He was heard to remark, "I'm afraid Jimmie won't have a car much longer if he ever lets a woman behind the wheel." Many years later, when he visited us in Southern Ontario, he used to ride along with me whenever I drove out. He took back his words in his own inimitable way: "I just didn't know that women could drive as well as men."

Jim's grandfather, also named Jim Thaxter.

We all know what we have heard about husbands teaching their wives to drive. Things got a bit rocky at times – after a stint in the ditch, stalling half way up a steep hill, failed brakes and a blue haze around the car when Jim was not happy with my efforts – but we both thought I was ready to try for my license.

Note: Believe it or not, our marriage lasted almost 35 years.

The roads where we lived were single lane; most places were wide enough to allow cars to meet, but there were many places where one of the drivers would have to back up to a wider space; hopefully not me. Also, using the horn liberally as you went round a bend was a must.

Just before I was going to apply for my license, Jim had a break down on the binder. He asked me to drive in to town and pick up the needed part. I was hesitant about not having my license, but Police were not as rigid about regulations then; if you explained the circumstances, they would most likely accept the situation. Besides in a small place, everyone knew everyone else.

I was very nervous. I had my two-year-old daughter in the car; no seat belts in those days. I started the six miles to town at about 20 miles per hour; when I was about half way there, I forgot to be nervous, and souped it up to 25. Nothing to it, I thought.

Well, pride goeth before a fall. About two miles from town, there was a long low hill. About half way up, the car stalled and I couldn't even pull off to the side. When I climbed out to look, one front tire was headed west and the other was headed north. I stood there perplexed, as I had never seen anything like this before.

I was soon joined by a neighbour, who was just home from the Singapore prison camp. He looked things over and remarked: "Is Jim trying to kill you or is he just scaring you to death?" He laughed then and told me that someone had been working on the car and had left out a vital bolt in the steering column. "Not to worry, Vern," he said, "I will have it fixed in a jiffy." He went over to the fence he had been repairing, cut off a piece of wire, returned, and had the car going in a very few minutes. There were a few dangerous spots on that road, and I was lucky the car had stopped where it did.

Now I was nervous! I drove around each block in town rather than trying to back up to turn. I did my sedate 20 miles per hour on the way home, where I accosted my husband. He turned absolutely white. There had been three of them working on the car the evening before, and each one thought the other had put in the vital bolt. I could understand the mistake, but I didn't intend to let him forget it too soon!

Our nearest town to apply for a driving test was fifteen miles away. Jim's friend was the proprietor of the shop. I don't know how he ever received or held down that post as he was

Verna's brother-in-law, Bernie Streich's 1930 Buick and her father-in-law's 1930 Chev at her old home.

Left to right, Harold Grant, Verna and Jim (before their marriage). In the background is Jim's 1929 Chev that he traded for a cow when Verna and Jim started to farm.

mostly referred to as "that crazy dumbbell". When in Espanola one day, Jim ran into him on the street. "I am going to bring my wife in for her driver's test one of these days." Jim told him. "Is she a good driver?" he asked. "Of course she is," Jim replied, lying through his teeth.

"Well, come on in and I'll fix her up right now." Crazy Dumbbell lived up to his name. Without ever seeing me, or my driving, he filled in the forms and presented Jim with my Driver's License.

Needless to say I was ecstatic when Jim arrived home and gave me the news. But I was a little let down when I read on the forms that I was now five years older than I was that morning; Jim had given his own age instead of mine. It took me eight years to rectify that error. It only came to mind when I was applying for a renewal, and I was just laughed at when I wanted it changed. However, in Port Perry, I found one kind hearted man who believed me and corrected the error.

THE DUO

After the war, we were still struggling with a shortage of machinery and other things. We had, still, the horse we had been given and a spare one from my father-in-law, Bob. Now Bob needed his horse. After some discussion, Jim decided to get another horse. There was a dealer coming into town with a truckload of horses.

Jim attended the sale and arrived home with not one but two horses. They were a beautiful pair of three-year-old Belgians, a black and a white. Jim was so excited he could hardly speak; he had fallen madly and irrevocably in love with them. I asked him why he bought two. "You know, Vern," he answered, "They were sisters and I couldn't make up my mind, nor could I separate them."

We sold the spare horse and settled down with Beauty and Silver. They were his pride and joy and his loves for the rest of their lives. I am quite convinced that had he to make a choice between the horses, or myself, they would have won hands (or hooves) down over me.

These two ladies were real workers and an asset to any farmer; and of course Jim used them like the beauties they were. Nothing was too good for them. He bought iron from the Watkins dealer, special mixes to add to their grain and anything else that he thought might enhance them. For a treat, he boiled potatoes, and sometimes a meal of boiled grain. Every meal had an additive. The result of this was that the horses were working on a high at all times. They were, at times, almost uncontrollable. Runaways were the way of life for Jim and his ladies.

One winter day, we had gone into town for supplies. With us were my sister-in-law, Phyllis, and her son Bobbie. Just as we were leaving for home, the horses decided it was time to leave. Jim was not quite ready, and when they left, they pulled one rein out of his hand. We went bouncing around town over sidewalks, snow banks and in some cases, almost over people. When finally he had them in control, he had a very red face, and four very frightened people aboard.

Another time, he was alone in town when they took the bit in their teeth and ran. This time they ended up with the tongue of the sleigh stuck fast in the wall of a friend's house. Bernice was doing dishes at the window and almost died of fright when the team ran into the house.

There was a rumour in Webbwood that when Jim and his high stepping horses were in town, every one left the streets until he had left for home.

The day after our son was born, Jim was probably not so careful because he had been up all night with my mother waiting for me to produce his son. This day they ran away with the rake and dragged him along too, leaving him with scrapes and bruises all over his body. Each year, as long as he lived, on Warren's birthday, July 10, he kept that story alive by telling and retelling the story.

When we moved to Southern Ontario, they moved along with us. When the trucks, bringing our furniture and machinery were immobile in mud, Jim harnessed the horses and they pulled the truck free. They would work their hearts out for him.

Marilyn was not a horse person, so she liked it much better when we acquired a tractor. But Warren learned to ride on them. They hold many memories for him.

We always had a large acreage of root vegetables, which were cultivated by a scuffler. Jim took turns using the horses. When he used Beauty, Silver stayed contentedly in the other pasture. But when he used Silver, Beauty always jumped the fence and walked all day side by side, unharnessed beside Silver. He eventually just turned Beauty loose when it was not her turn, because she would get there eventually anyway. When he brought them in from pasture, he had only to lead one of them; the other would follow.

Silver was struck with lightning while in the pasture. Beauty was a long time recovering from her loss. She would come up to the barn and keep calling, hoping her mate would answer from inside the stable. Beauty was sold at our sale when we left Greenbank. Jim mourned for her when she left; it was like losing one of the family.

BARBED WIRE

"I heard some interesting news today." Jim had just come home from town and was telling me a piece of most interesting news.

It was 1947. Everything was tight still from the war. There were so many things wanted, such as farming machinery, household goods and cars, but still were unavailable. Fencing was another thing in short supply. In Espanola, where the Prisoners of War had been held, the barracks were surrounded by barbed wire; miles and miles of it lying unused, but not one yard of it could be bought in the stores. Earlier that year, the Government had given orders to get rid of it, but made no suggestions as to how it should be done. It would be a very costly thing to do if they had to pay some one to do it. Finally someone came up with the suggestion that they just give it away to anyone who would take it. Luckily, Jim was in town and heard about it right away.

He would need help if he were to take on the job. That evening he went to see our closest neighbour, Gerry. He wondered if the two of them could have a go at it. No Thaxter was ever accused of having poor fences. We were having a hard time making do with what materials we had, so the barbed wire was a real perk. Sure enough, Gerry was willing to help. Neither owned a car, so we had to borrow my father-in-law's.

It was well below zero weather, in late January, when they tackled it. They had to wear their worst clothes, as they knew that barbed wire would wreck them. They took their lunch with them and made tea and coffee over a fire. The frozen sandwiches had to be toasted before being eaten.

The first day they were very discouraged, as they couldn't seem to find a beginning place for the wire. The next day was a bit better, but still not good. By the third day, they were well into it and could really peel it off. As the news leaked out, many others came for the wire. Quite a few never came back after the first day. A few others kept on tenaciously.

With a couple of days off here and there, they worked for two weeks. Each day they brought home their hard-earned rolls of wire on a wagon behind the car. The wickedly cold weather held, all of the time they were working there. Of course it turned mild after the dirty job was done.

While working, they found many traces of tunnels, which had been started and abandoned, where the prisoners had made plans to escape. Some of them were successful; but apparently all of the escapees were returned. The land was very sandy and light. The camp was right on the banks of the Spanish River, so they tried tunnelling down and came out on the steep banks below the dam.

Espanola had been, and still is, a mill town. There had been a dam built on the Spanish, which was responsible for the beginning of the town.

It was common, in the war years, to drive into Espanola and see a gang of prisoners in special clothes with large red circles on the back. They exercised the prisoners for road repairs, etc.

It was a back-breaking job, but both of the men were very happy with their supply of wire. It sure beat paying out money, which none of us had, if the wire had been available in the stores.

MOVING DAY

A vacation from the farm in the forties was just out of the question; the stock and the crops always had to be tended. But in late summer of 1950, we found some reliable farm help and decided to take a few days and see how the other half lived in Southern Ontario. So far neither of us had been more than a hundred miles from home, and of course we had never left Ontario.

We had some friends in Southern Ontario and an invitation to visit them, so we decided to go for a short visit.

Highway 69 was not opened yet, so the only route was to go east from Sudbury to North Bay, and then south on Highway 11. After seeing the wide open, beautiful farms there, we immediately fell in love with the country, and I have never yet lost my love for it.

We had only about forty acres of tillable land on our present farm. It had more bush and rocks than fields. The rocks were always hidden out of sight, and were there when there was a well or fence posts to be dug; or when digging a foundation for a building. The last couple of years we rented another farm and we worked the fields of both. We knew if we were able to make a move, it had to be soon as we were not getting any younger.

On our arrival back home, we put all of our efforts into making the move. Our farm was put up for sale. After a couple of quick return visits, we finally found a farm that winter that we could afford. The only fly in the ointment was that we could not find a buyer for our farm. After much careful thought, we made a big decision and bought it anyway. Oh Lord, didn't we have nerve to just walk away from this one and never look back! About a year and a half later, after our move, we sold the farm.

We immediately started selling what we were not taking with us. It was hard knowing we were leaving our families and all of our lifetime friends. We sold most of the stock and some bulky machinery. These could be replaced down there. After arranging for a railroad car to transport some of our things, there was still a truckload of stock to come in a couple of days. Jim, of course, took his beloved horses on the railroad car. Moving that far was a costly business.

To ship live stock this distance, someone had to travel with them to feed and water them. Jim agreed to go alone with the stock. A young neighbour of ours was going to Toronto, so he agreed to help me drive down with the two kids.

After the move to town with the things we were shipping, we stayed overnight in Massey with my sister and her family. Jim had to leave shortly after midnight; we left around 8:00 a.m.

We owned a 1931 Ford, and left with every inch of space full; of course there were no trunks in those old cars. We had our luggage, plus Lorne's (the neighbour who was helping me).

It was early in April and had been raining for days. When we were about twenty miles from Sudbury we hit our first problem. The Vermilion River had flooded its banks. The road had been closed the day before. It was much higher than a car could cross. There was such a line up of vehicles wanting over, that the Department of Highways allowed one of their large trucks to tow each one across. When it was our turn, we scrambled up on the seats, and put our luggage, and everything we could pile up away from the water. We looked in dismay at the floor mats rising and wondered just how far they would continue.

Safely across on the other side, we had to wait for the wires to dry before the car would start. There was some damage to the lights, but after stopping at a couple of garages, they said they couldn't fix it. One of them gave us a name in North Bay and assured us that it could be done there. The next day, they closed the road. It was another week before the truckload of stock arrived.

We made it to North Bay, and left the car in the garage for the needed repairs while we had lunch in a nearby restaurant. We went on our way with the lights back to normal. The children had been exceptionally quiet all the way. Marilyn was two and a half, and was always a quiet child, while Warren was almost seven and a real "heller". But during this move he was showing his very best side. He was very quiet and subdued. I know that Marilyn was too young to understand, but Warren had moved from the only home he had ever known and must have been full of apprehensions. We arrived at our friends' place late in the evening. During the whole trip, those two kids were unbelievably good. I had never heard even one cry from them that day. We would be going over to the new farm in the morning, but right now, we were too weary to care.

Meantime, back at the railroad, the agent at Massey had booked the car all the way C.P.R., instead of switching at Sudbury to C.N.R. Meanwhile the car went over to Lindsay, Peterborough, and Heaven knows where else, before arriving in Blackwater. It should have arrived on Thursday, but had been shunted aside a couple of times and didn't arrive until noon Friday.

The trucks that we had arranged to transfer our things to the farm got stuck in the very muddy lane. Jim just harnessed Beauty and Silver and towed them out. Of course, it didn't make any hard feelings when he kept hearing some of the movers admiring the way the horses had worked when almost flat out. Jim expected a lot from that team and they never disappointed him.

Joyce Withers
Bought in Massey Museum
July 6/002